Shebeen Tales

CHENJERAI HOVE, one of Zimbabwe's leading writers, was born in 1956. His novels include *Bones*, which won the 1989 Noma Award for Publishing in Africa, and *Shadows*, and he has also written poetry and radio plays. His work has been translated into German, Dutch, Danish, Swedish, Norwegian and Japanese.

BY THE SAME AUTHOR

Fiction
Masimba Avanhu?
Bones
Shadows

Poetry
Red Hills of Home

Shebeen Tales

Messages from Harare

Chenjerai Hove

Serif
London

Baobab Books
Harare

This edition first published 1994 by
Serif
47 Strahan Road
London E3 5DA

and in Southern Africa by
Baobab Books
PO Box 1559
Harare
(a division of Academic Books (Pvt) Ltd, Harare)

Originally published, in slightly different form,
in Dutch as *Berichten uit Harare* by
In de Knipscheer, Amsterdam, 1993

British Library Cataloguing-in-Publication Data.
A catalogue record for this book
is available from the British Library.

ISBN 1 897959 16 8

Photoset in North Wales by
Derek Doyle & Associates, Mold, Clwyd
Printed and bound in Great Britain by
Biddles of Guildford

Contents

Prologue

As a Dutch publisher of many African authors, including Zimbabwe's Chenjerai Hove, I visited him in Harare towards the end of 1991 at the International Zimbabwe Book Fair which he had helped to organise. There I commissioned him to write a series of essays to be published in *De Volkskrant*, the Amsterdam daily paper, and later in book form by In de Knipscheer. We agreed that I in turn would write a column for the Zimbabwean newspaper *Horizon* about my experiences as an outsider in Harare, alternating with reports of my conversations with Chenjerai. The publication of the English-language edition of *Shebeen Tales* seemed an appropriate occasion to use my pieces for *Horizon* as a prologue to Chenjerai's collected newspaper columns.

Chenjerai Hove writes his essays from the inside out; they are fluent impressions of Harare. He often quotes the work of his fellow writers, not merely because literature in Zimbabwe often cuts close to the bone of reality but also because he does not want to make any distinction between facts and fiction, feeling and intellect.

Hove has woven the themes of his fiction into his columns: the war of independence, the theatre of power, nostalgia for the land, alienation in the city, the experience of nature, tangible memory and intangible reality. All these subjects are explored in literary and emotional depth in his novels. These columns are the quickly jotted daily observations in the margins of his lyrical novels.

Since becoming the capital of an independent Zimbabwe in 1980, Harare's town planning has remained reminiscent of the Salisbury of Ian Smith. People now live mixed together in what were once neighbourhoods for 'coloureds', blacks or whites, but the luxurious suburbs studded with mansions surrounded by walls and immense, constantly-watered, well-kept gardens alternate with golf courses, providing a striking green contrast to the surrounding dry landscape.

At half past six in the morning the sun is shining, huge and round, above the blue trees in blossom along Selous Avenue. Bumper to bumper Harare's motorists are heading for work on the slick paved streets. Thick throngs of humanity scurry along the pavements and through parks on their way to shopping centres and offices of glass and steel.

People form orderly queues to buy the morning paper at the news-stand. Long strings of passengers lengthen at bus-stops, many waiting to be taken to businesses where they will be given a couple of hours of casual manual labour.

By eight o'clock the papers are sold out, the buses have gone and casual labour has all been assigned. Left to the news on the radio, the luck of hitching a ride and the hope of work tomorrow, the queues of people dissolve in the glitter and the luxury of the city centre.

The centre of Harare is still divided into sections with mathematical precision. First, Second, Third and Fourth Streets intersect avenues laid at right angles to them. Urban life within these cool and efficient quadrants makes an empty impression unlike most other African cities with their explosions of colour, maze of streets, fragrant aromas and lively street trade.

One evening I'm basking in the soothing sounds of human voices at the Terreskane bar, where men down one bottle of beer after another. I'm sitting at one of the few tables that still has a tablecloth. Music blends with the sound of bottles plonking on tables. A man is standing in front of me, chewing the last bits of meat and wiping his hands on my tablecloth. Suddenly there's a commotion, the Terreskane security people have discovered a man carrying a loaded revolver. In another corner two boys face each other in a karate stance, their torsos huffing and puffing in macho style before they embrace amid cackles of their own laughter.

An old man comes up to me. Afraid his brimming, loosely held glass of beer might spill on my white suit, I offer him a chair. He plops right down. He was trained in the revolutionary army in Mozambique by Yugoslavs and Russians. He had fought for many years. Now he is alone with his memories of comradeship and the reasons behind the struggle. Laughter and crying resound from three tables further on. The man drops his glass and it smashes to pieces.

The Terreskane is full to the brim. I work on my notes, girls tittering 'dream guy' at me but leaving me in peace. In a corner a fat cook is grilling slabs of meat and flies are buzzing around a generous bowl of salad. A drunk approaches me.

'You're tired?'

'No, it's OK.'

'They bothering you?'

'No, it's fine.'

He raises his arms, his motor co-ordination gone.

'Don't let nobody ever give you shit, man.' He stumbles away, turns and, almost singing, says, 'You are Zimbabwean. You are a man.'

Suddenly I feel a lot less tired.

'Pssst. Can I have one more beer?'

'*Ndinotenda!* (Thanks!)'

Chenjerai talks as he drives me around the city. 'The land has value and the personality that we call our own. Cities in Southern Africa are designed to work and sleep in. The city does not make up any part of the human soul. That has not changed since independence. For most of us, the land is a symbol of fertility, continuity and renewal. The land is an extension of our soul. Our culture is much more connected to the land, the earth, the seasons, than it is to the city that is geared for work and profit. Many songs are sung about people refusing to be buried in the city because they have no relationship to it, they do not experience it as their own or belonging to life. When we die the soul must find the peace of the land. You indicate in advance the spot at which you wish to be buried. A spot that can never be replaced by highly organised urban churchyards which are cut off from real life.'

We pick our way through the traffic that drives on the left side of the road. Suddenly everything comes to a halt. Amid motorcycles and shrieking sirens the presidential limousine flashes past.

'What are they all so afraid of, Africa's leaders?' Hove sighs. 'They lose all contact with reality. All their power does is move the air. So often, they're prisoners trapped in a fiction of fear and power. The arrogance of power: one loses grip on reality.'

A song jumps out of the car radio released the day after a horrible bus accident in which 30 people were killed:

Bus-driver, oh bus-driver, drive carefully, please.
Think about those whose life is in your hands.

There are large numbers of fatal accidents caused by rickety overloaded vehicles and drunken bus-drivers.

Chenjerai's mother is staying with him and sits watching a science-fiction movie with his children playing at her feet. Her grandchildren are not interested in her stories which Hove fed on during his childhood and which formed the basis of his feeling for words and his becoming a writer. She looks at the English-language film, not understanding a word.

An item on the news covers the cotton harvest. She sits up straight at the sight of the villages. In the mean time Chenjerai complains about the colonial inheritance of having to plant cotton for the world market instead of agricultural products for local consumption. 'You can't eat cotton. And we don't get a good enough price for cotton to buy enough food at the market.'

His mother watches the images of the village pushed aside again, this time for an American sitcom with canned laughter taking place in a kitchen which to her must look as if it came from another planet.

'We live here for the most part in an oral world whose daily organisation is ruled by the written word,' Chenjerai observes. 'The names of streets are written, offices function thanks to the written word ... When I walk with my mother through the city I feel the tragic gap between her world and the new surroundings governed by the written word. I feel her loneliness in a world in which all doors are locked by the English language and behavioural codes.

'I consider illiteracy as a form of censorship. Of course I am also aware that mastery of the written language can destroy a lot of the power of imagination in using language. But I deplore the tragedy of someone who does not stand with feet in both the spoken and written word.'

We discuss language, the distinction between fiction and non-fiction, literature and history, imagination and reality, and I mention something the Brazilian author João Ubaldo Ribeiro once said, 'The secret of truth is that facts do not exist, only stories.'

'I am a poet in my bones,' Chenjerai replies, 'but I also write radio plays, stage plays, novels, stories and articles. I'm constantly looking for a better form in which to interpret human experience. I write both in Shona, my mother tongue, and in English. You relate to and experience the world through language. I also speak Ndebele and continue to experience how existence is seen and dreamed from the point of view of this language. For me languages are schools of life.

'In my work there is constant conversation between the earth, nature and the sky. As far as I'm concerned, this communication only really occurs when I work in Shona. The person who gets the dialogue going between the earth, the sky and humans, ancestors and the gods — no matter where you are in the world — is the story-teller. He or she is a philosopher, a master of language. You can only become a master of language if you grasp experience, that is, from both sides of the visible world. Language gives you the possibility of expressing what you know and of gathering together all the social and natural powers to make things understandable to people who you are directly involved with and with whom you want to create a dialogue.

'We must abandon the notion that literature is only written on the page. It can also be recorded on the roll of memory. Master story-tellers can always breathe new life into a story depending on the circumstances in which they tell it. History is generally seen as a summation of facts. I see history as slices of experience which we digest in our novels and poems.

'Just imagine for a moment that the world could be stopped for two hours and that you yourself could summon up experiences in the calm of the everyday storm. Memories do not well up chronologically, they are associative. Memories cut right across linear time and colour events and facts from the point of view of various imaginative and emotional palettes, depending on the emotion of the moment. Facts do not exist, only different stories. History is comprised of desperation, hope, life, fear, death, feelings that are very hard to depict in fiction, let alone in a history book. From the perspective of various worlds of experience all experience casts shadows on the different moments of memory.

'This multi-dimensional experience should be simultaneously danced, sung, written, painted and sculpted. On its own, a novel can never finish a story. Experiencing facts escapes your grasp when you put them down on paper. You are only able to catch a glimpse of a few hues of motley reality by engaging in a dialogue of the culture with itself.

'I believe that fiction is a very thin slice of reality. So much happens in a human life. When we try to depict this in our stories, it will inevitably look more like fiction than reality. But fiction does not exist. I don't want to keep fiction and reality apart. Human beings are very complex animals. Our decisions, feelings and experiences are determined by our wishes, legends and the past. I believe, by the way, that people themselves are bits of imagination. We are invented. We are invented by other people. Others have dreamed about us, we ourselves are a dream, a shadow of the past. Long ago my ancestors dreamed of me. In that way they took care of the continuity of existence.

'Every human is driven by the same question: Who will make sure that my blood continues to flow, that my breath will not fail? Even my own breath is fiction, is imagined by someone else. The air that fills my lungs has been blown here from thousands of years ago. In any event I don't rack my brains worrying about the separation between fiction and reality. Fiction is our reality. Reality is our imagination.'

The next day I take a taxi to Mbare, one of Harare's oldest townships. The driver and I are talking about books. No, he cannot spend money on books.

'Too dear.'

Could it just be a matter of choice between a book or having a few beers?

'No, books are too expensive, and besides there are no books I can really curl up with.'

My mind is swept clean by Mbare's music, dust, crowds, roaring buses and aromas from the market. Until I reach the spot where people have constructed makeshift houses out of rubbish. A grey sea of hundreds of shelters knocked together out of cardboard, plastic and newspapers, rippling between the market and the traffic lights efficiently channelling the stream of cars into the inner city.

Do people live here, fifteen minutes of immaculately paved road away from one of the most modern African cities? I decide to ask a man I spot reading an English-language textbook. He offers me a beer.

Yes, he lives here with his wife and children. There is no more work on the land and now no job in the city or financial support from the government, despite his long years of service in the liberation army. We start talking about the novels I have read that deal with the war, such as Hove's *Bones* and Chinodya's *Harvest of Thorns*. Did he know them?

'Yes, heard of them, vaguely, but too expensive to buy.'

Coming from him, I believed it.

A short time later I am gliding back to the other world of the city centre and ask to be dropped off at the Sheraton Hotel whose gilded edifice towers above Harare. In the bar a dulcet-toned singer accompanies himself on a synthesiser. Two whites in short trousers that are too long ask me whether I am enjoying Rhodesia and whether I think Salisbury is a beautiful city.

There's a cynical irony to Zimbabwe's book trade. People crave reading material. They queue to buy an affordable newspaper, printed in insufficient numbers because of a shortage of paper. Imported books are too expensive for most readers because of the import tariffs while the local publishing industry is stagnating because of that very same paper shortage. Beneath the double layer of irony, indirect censorship lies in wait for writing which examines the current yawning social gap between rich and poor and which as a result will never see the light of day.

The common denominator of the African book industry, despite social, cultural or technical differences, was brought home to me by a taxi driver and township dweller: there is no inexpensive, popular literature available where readers turn the pages to the heartbeat of this life. So therefore these kinds of books should also be made available outside normal bookshops. They should be on hand at the heart of the life from which they are written, amid the music and rumbling buses, shoulder to shoulder with maize and tomatoes, on the heads of the boys and girls that bob behind crowded bus windows, laden with eggs, biscuits and fruit but, as far as I have seen, no … books.

One evening I go out with a couple of people to a township. The night club is a bare space with wooden tables, a bar and a kitchen. The band plays non-stop from nine in the evening to four in the morning. Music gives time wings. Men dance with one another. Women dance with one another. Sometimes they mix. Dance, dance, dance. Alone with the music. Hardly any talk. One remark keeps coming back to mind: 'We are in shit, man. Deep shit. Come on, dance, man. Dance!'

'The writer must keep on dreaming for his society,'

Chenjerai Hove observes. 'Not many people listen to the echoes of their dreams in the morning. Most dreams in this world do not receive attention, they are slowly abandoned to the warpaths of this life. The poet has to come to grips, do battle with these dreams, reminding the dreamers they have a right to their own dreams. Their dreams deserve a spot on the map of the world.

'The writer is a map-maker. The history of each society is better understood with the help of its artistic products. In hard times the artist will blend images of despair with those of hope. In good times the writer will depict the madness of over-eating at the expense of cultivating other values.'

Jan Kees van de Werk

Harare's High Fences, Neighbours and Dogs

The American poet Robert Frost thought that, 'Good fences make good neighbours.' Of course, he was also right in asking who you are shutting out and who are you shutting in. But my mother does not think Robert Frost was right. 'Who are your neighbours?' she once asked when we had moved into a new house, our own.

High walls, neighbours and dogs, they all came to my mind as I tried to look for satisfactory answers to her question. She usually does not want her questions evaded, even with wit and sharp turns and twists of the language. Still she came back to her question after listening 'intently' to my stories of digression ... goats, sheep, schoolchildren and their lazy ways, and all that.

'I said, who are your neighbours?' she insisted.

But then, how do I tell her about the new happenings of the city where high walls, barking hounds and warnings on gates are a common presence? 'Beware of the dog' say most entrances to houses in the city's good suburbs. Usually the owners of the house mean it, with huge hounds barking like lions from inside the high walls of the 'fenced and gated' house.

'When selling a house, it always makes a difference if the house is "fenced and gated". That is my trade, knowing what kind of house sells,' says the estate agent, proudly too. He has the market at his fingertips. The nuances of selling a house in Harare are part of his acquired 'knowledge', the type you don't ever see on anyone's certificate. 'Gated and fenced' can put up the price of a house by tens of thousands of dollars.

'Walls and gates remind me of prison,' a Zimbabwean writer, Dambudzo Marechera, once said. As for dogs and their barking, I don't know what he would have said. But certainly, the barking of dogs in Harare is one of its most recent nocturnal orchestras, with an invisible conductor: the intruder in the night.

Yes, when they say 'Beware of the dog' this is not an overstatement. Don't expect a puppy to sneak out of the gate to come and lick your shoes for fun. My nine-year-old son discovered this the hard way in a hospital being tested for rabies after a vicious dog bite tore his knee. The notice was there, but the boy was too anxious to reach out for the other boys playing inside the neighbours' yard to read it before trying to open the gate. A few seconds later he was screaming, and the neighbours brought out documents to show that the dog was indeed vaccinated against rabies. The wife was frantic, cursing and shouting at me for not keeping my children to myself, in my own yard. Now the boy responds to the 'Beware of the dog' signs.

Dogs and neighbours may not have much in common, but in Harare they are behind a high fence, a wall recently built by the many mushrooming companies whose adverts on TV always remind you of how unsafe you are until you are walled in.

'Walled and gated, that's your safety,' one slogan says.

So, up to now, my only neighbour is one without a wall, like me. Yes, we both have dogs, but no walls. He is a sculptor and hates walls. I am a writer and I hate walls. 'We have to cut a hole in this fence, our children should be able to jump through the fence and play,' he said the other day. I always agree with such venturesome suggestions, but a friend soon arrived, with a friend of a friend of a friend who earns his living by installing fences, burglar bars and thief-tight car sheds.

'If you are security-conscious, you will need all these things,' says the other guy. Then I recall Robert Frost's line, 'Good fences make good neighbours,' and I think, 'Good fences make no neighbours at all.'

Meanwhile, the wall construction business thrives, and the adverts on radio and television remind Harareans how unsafe they are until they have walls around their houses. Unfortunately, the television adverts appear on the only channel which everyone watches. So, I say to myself, we are all insecure.

Maybe I should change Frost's lines and say, 'Good fences make frightened citizens.'

The dog selling business must be doing well too, as well as the wall construction business. The other day we had a stunning message on the screen of our only telex machine. 'Hi there. Do you feel unsafe and alone in the house? We are selling a female puppy. Telephone now if you need it.' Maybe good puppies make good neighbours.

A friend put up a 'Beware of the dog' sign soon after buying a puppy, and when I got there I looked around for the dog and found none. Then at lunch the little guard appeared, sniffing around and mewing like a cat, completely helpless. Good puppies may make good neighbours.

At the Society for the Prevention of Cruelty to Animals potential dog-owners queue in search of the dog to assist the wall in protecting the family. On the radio, announcers shout every day about the missing dog, or the wanted dog or the stray dog which responds to some name or other: Pinky, Tanya, even Pauline, or — surprisingly — John. Why not name the dog Peter, the Rock, I asked a friend who had a vicious dog which would not allow you near the gate twenty-four hours a day.

How many dogs are in the city, Harare, I once asked a government vet at a cocktail party. 'Oh,' he said, 'that is a good question. As many dogs as there are people. One to one,' he laughed.

The other day, news about a dog restaurant stole the show in the main evening news. I phoned to protest.

'What do Zimbabweans have to do with American dog restaurants?' I screamed. The voice at the other end was calm and composed. 'What you might not know is that there is a large enough population of dogs here to warrant ten restaurants,' he said.

As for the amounts spent on dogs and other pets, I do not have the statistics. But it is rumoured that a good dog-owner spends more on his dog than on the domestic servant. Recently there was talk of introducing a medical aid scheme for dogs, even though there is no medical scheme for most workers, and the wall construction business must grab millions of dollars from the purses of security-conscious Harareans.

And the formerly illegal dog races are soon to be introduced in Zimbabwe when the law forbidding the sport as cruel is repealed. There will be dog races and the adverts will probably be amended accordingly: 'Dog for protection — and for the races.' Soon Harareans will be watching dog races, alongside horse races, alongside human races, before retreating behind the walls of the new security of Harare with its non-existent neighbours.

'First World', 'Third World' and 'Fourth World' City

'Welcome to the city of Harare' the city fathers wrote on a large, beautiful signpost near the airport, positioned close to the independence arch carved out of some of the most expensive marble there is. The city of Harare indeed. If I were a city father, I would have written 'Welcome to the cities of Harare', for there are many cities in one, with different flavours, or personalities, if you want to put it that way.

'First World', 'Second World', 'Third World', those are the sections of this capital of nearly a million people, including the homeless who tend to settle on any open space available. They do so, creating another, maybe 'Fourth' or 'Fifth World'. But the police always get there sooner or later, with batons and handcuffs in their hands, to erase the squatter camps with the anger of fire if not bulldozers. That is probably their only way into the newspapers, the squatters whom no one claims as their relatives.

The inner city, the glamorous one where everyone wants to be, including the youth of the so-called 'nose brigade', those who try to speak English like 'real Englishmen' and 'Englishwomen'. They are here too, eating chicken and chips in the mushrooming 'fast food' shops designed and organised like any in London or New York. They are all here, in the centre of the real life of the city as dreamt many years ago by planners who saw this city as a mini-London or New York or Tokyo.

This is the 'First World' part of the city, with flashy cars, smartly dressed men and women purposefully rushing to some unknown nowhere at an incredible speed. The expensive cars, the flower-boys selling roses, the glittering shops well-fitted with neon lights to dazzle the night shopper, they are all here, then the wide streets, broad and clean, in which even a blind man could drive, for they are straight and arranged neatly in a pattern in which it is hard for anyone to get lost.

'First World' Harare is also where the expensive hotels are, demanding a jacket and tie even for a passer-by wanting to taste the rich Tanganda tea from the Eastern Highlands whose 'taste says share it', as the advertisements claim. As for wearing jeans in these hotels, forget it. Food vendors, those selling juicy oranges but without the advantage of a shop, are arrested and carted away, like sheep to the slaughter. Never mind, I say to myself, if I can't buy the nice oranges today, I will buy some tomorrow, as the 'illegal vendors' always seem to find a way of intruding into the unadulterated 'First World' Harare where they are not wanted.

I do not shop in 'First World' Harare, but I go there anyway, to compare the prices, to locate what I want. 'First World' Harare, with its many fascinations, has the most expensive of anything. Ironically, there is 'First' Street, the busiest shopping centre of the city, crowded but clean. Cleaners are there all the time, engaged in incessant battle with dust and the occasional leaf, plus the left-overs from those who pay homage to the inventor of 'fast food' with its 'fast garbage'.

It is in First Street that I hear so many choruses, as if a church choir has just begun its choral and serene appeal to the gods for mercy or for plenty. The beggars of the city are here, singing, with their children playing around, jumping all over the place, but not too far away from the melody of the blind mother or father whom they must lead away when the sun threatens to abandon them.

'Lord, the merciful one, help me like you helped the children of Israel,' sings one. 'Oh Lord, have pity on me, Lord have pity on me, I am shattered by problems,' shouts another: always that one song for busy 'First World' Harare.

Harareans pass by without noticing, obsessed with their destinations. An occasional lonely coin tinkles on the plate firmly gripped by the starved and pitiable hands of the blind or the destitute. Beggars beggars beggars, in the glamour of the city.

The chorusing beggars know it might not be long before the 'city fathers' clean the city as they often do. They occasionally do so with police vans and the fire brigade, bundling beggars into vans before carting them to some unknown destination. Never mind, I console myself, they will come back, one day. And they do, always.

In 'First World' Harare the blind sit along the pavements, the destitute blessed with eyesight carry their belongings along, in the clean street, evoking the nightmarish image of the very clean against the background of the very neglected. They carry ragged newspapers, old clothes washed I don't know when and headloads of other unimaginable objects, begging if they can, scrounging in a nearby dustbin, not upsetting it for fear of annoying the authorities.

Sometimes the newspapers notice them, but most of the time they don't. The other day one found a thrilling hobby which got newspaper coverage. He took to removing all the parking tickets stuck under the windscreen wipers of motorists who had over-stayed their parking times.

Then there is another destitute, right in the middle of the street, with bundles of everything and a well-posted sign reading 'This property managed by Knight Frank and Rutley', one of the most successful real estate companies in the country. The road is named after former president of Tanzania, Julius Nyerere, it used to be Kingsway, but now it is Julius Nyerere Way, dissecting the city from north to south into eastern and western halves, the 'First World' and the 'Third World' of Harare.

Near Julius Nyerere Way, people wear different clothes and the houses are more makeshift at times, with a touch of individual fingers where bank loans ran short. But across on the other side of the road the shops are crowded, the people are less aware of themselves, their pace is rugged and the streets are narrow and neglected. Even the language is rougher, people are not happy to call a spade a digging instrument. Push someone out of the bus queue and you hear, 'Hey, this is not your mother's bus.'

A pair of shoes which only a few seconds ago would have cost me 120 Zimbabwean dollars can all of a sudden be 60 dollars. A shirt which was 100 dollars on the other side suddenly becomes 30 dollars, a bargain price, and the shop owners, mostly of Indian origin and unsmiling, do not always insist on their prices. '*Buya tinapangana* (Come, let us discuss the price)', they say. Usually they employ someone to stand by the door, urging and cajoling customers to 'come in and see'. And when the price is not right, I can always say, no, this is too much. The usual plea is, 'How much do you have?' and the bargaining starts in earnest.

In this 'Third World' Harare, the cars swerve and miss each other by a few inches, with a wave of the hand for an apology or simply the car horn. The smashed body-work of the cars and drivers wearing anything which happened to be near to hand that morning, they all tell me, in the words of Zimbabwean poet Musa Zimunya, 'Never mind brother, this is our home.' Indeed this is my home, and life goes on.

If I fall hungry and my tummy demands its share of earthly pleasures, the small cafés offer me the local maize meal lunch, with beef and vegetables, at one dollar fifty cents, no jacket or tie or jeans or anything on the entrance rules.

Life in the 'Third World' part reminds me that this is not the world of business executives, it is the world of those who see life 'face to face', as the locals say. Or those who came to the city 'too look for a morsel'. The business executives only pass through, on their way to the industrial sites, to check on their goods manufactured for export. Should I wave to a business executive driving past, I know I will be ignored.

'No beggars here' and 'No hawkers' notices always threaten on the front doors of 'First World' Harare. But 'Third World' Harare does not mind. Beggars and hawkers are not a problem there. They do not bother. 'How can the poor beg from the poor?' says a friend talking about the economics of begging and illegal selling.

So the beggars swarm across 'First World' Harare, with its glitter and glimmer of goods so highly priced that only those who do not bother about the contents of their purses dare to buy. Not so with 'Third World' Harare, the city of narrow streets and winding roads intertwined into Joseph Conrad's 'tangle of unrelated things'.

Then a further walk, down the road, towards Harare's oldest suburb, Mbare. An old man is staggering from the pub on his way home. 'Everyone grew up here,' he shouts. 'Everyone including the politicians. I don't know why they never seem to get that straight,' he mumbles, speaking to me, to anyone who can hear, warning any potential ambushers that he is not quite 'drunk'. And I can hear his deep, rugged breath, striving to keep within him, the man whose only entertainment is a drinking bar where beer never runs short and I don't have to queue.

In this part of town, the 'African' one, everything is African. The language changes. No English, no nose brigades, no flashy window displays or cars. Everything is survival, and everything is there. The garages can fix your car, even on a Sunday, with makeshift spanners in a makeshift garage, while you wait.

The guy who makes sandals waits for me to change my old car tyre. He offers me a small amount to persuade me to part with it. He needs it in order to keep in business. 'Nothing for nothing,' he jokes, in the words of popular Zimbabwean musician, Thomas Mapfumo. 'Nothing for nothing is nothing,' the man quotes, rearranging his open shop of tyre sandals.

Tyre sandals are fashionable back home, and he works near the terminus for long-distance rural buses. He does not care about urban people. 'But sometimes they bring poor relatives to buy them cheap sandals.'

The rural buses are not like the 'express' type which stops at hotels and other fancy places in 'First World' Harare. Even when they are designed to carry 70 passengers, double that number is not too bad, as long as they are not caught by the police. The choruses of furious bus horns tell the intruder that here they mean business — they want passengers. And to get them they employ part-time assistants who, as soon as they see me, a potential passenger, dash up to me, singing praise to the virtues of the bus company, the courtesy, the low fares, the reliability of the conductors and drivers, the sweet music for those who want to dance on the spacious bus. But when you get in, you soon recall the folly of being taken in by poetry.

Poetry, life in this 'Third' or even 'Fourth' World Harare, everything is poetry. The vendor of oranges sings of oranges that speak, the herbalist sings of herbs that will make me more than fertile, the goods vendor wants to sell me handkerchiefs which will wipe my face on their own. Everything is alive in this part of the city — even the potatoes speak, so they say.

But I won't leave before I taste the local dish prepared in the open by women who run a co-operative in these parts. 'They used to be prostitutes,' says the man who points out the entrance of the place. 'But when they saw they were getting old and no man ran after them, they formed a co-operative. Now we run after them for food, not for anything else,' he laughs. And I know, although most of his teeth are missing, in this part of Harare he would never bother to buy artificial ones. His face is a piece of humour as it is, and the friends around him like him the way he is. They have nicknamed him 'the one with missing teeth'.

'First World' Harare, 'Third World' and 'Fourth

World' Harare, many cities in one city, and I wonder how it will end. Even though God created this city in 90 years, I don't know how I, the writer can repair it in my lifetime.

Song, Dance and Politics

The show begins with a song and, dreary though it may sound, I can see it is full of anticipation. As our people say, what is in the chest is hidden in a cave, no one can know. The songs well up with emotion and dance steps and gyrating waists add movement to song. The occasion: the president is arriving from another country.

> We have found the rock
> The rock to rule Zimbabwe
> We have found the rock
> The rock to rule Zimbabwe

the songstresses continue, in lullaby style at times, in serious mood at others, and the colours of their *kitenge* clothes bloom like human fireworks.

Often they talk of women in politics, on the African continent, in my country, Zimbabwe, in Malawi, even in Zaire. Women, the wretched of the earth, as Franz

Fanon put it. Women have been pushed off-stage for many years, and when the colonial experience came men were turned into migrant workers, leaving the women to control only the run-down rural areas where there was virtually nothing to control. Fortunately, my own father came back to the land before his old age to try to persuade the soil to give us life instead of giving it to his white boss who owned the mines and the farms.

Urban women run small organisations which are already marginalised for one reason or the other: the Women's Action Group, the Association of University Women (that is the 'fundis' or important people who teach at the university which is usually a male-dominated institution). Then there is the Association of Women's Clubs, barely visible but present. There are many more such crawling efforts by the women of the city, representing the women of the countryside, the illiterate for whom I thought I wrote my books until my own mother reminded me that what I write has nothing to do with her since she cannot read. 'Why don't you sit down and tell me the story?' she once said.

Then comes the conduct of the business of state, the realm of men. Women are there too, sometimes holding ministerial posts, sometimes in a huge parliament, fighting hard to be seen even as they swim against the flood of male political and social domination.

Politics, the art of ruling human beings, is not my realm. All I can do is to view, to see and warn, then remain silent. So much energy is spent barking up the wrong tree.

The only political pain I have, as a writer, is to see the women of my country in politics not as serious politicians, but as dancers, praise singers to the glory of the male politicians. They sing and dance, they kneel and make offerings in the manner of the traditional women of the village, paying homage to the glory of the man, with all the paraphernalia of water-pots, walking sticks and wooden plates.

The other day, at the airport, they were there when Nelson Mandela bid farewell to President Robert Mugabe and Vice-President Joshua Nkomo. The women took over the whole show, but away from the centre of the stage. The male dignitaries walked on the red carpet, feeling the praise songs and handclaps of the women seep through their ears to give them a vast sense of national and international stature. The women stood off the edge of the long red carpet, singing themselves hoarse, apparently happy to be onlookers to their own destiny.

I don't quite want to risk calling them 'airport women', but surprisingly when the male dignitaries arrive from or depart to nowhere, to somewhere, the women are there regardless of the time. They are there in their bright *kitenge* prints. They twist and sway with the spirit of dance, praising the immortal leader, the immortal Kamuzu or the ever-generous Mugabe …

All we have,
All we are,
Is because of you.

They sing, dance and go into frantic ululations, in praise of the god of the nation. Religious songs converted to the political realm. And I say to myself, 'We love to sing, we love to dance, we love to worship.'

Sing, dance, cry, worship. Africa is the centre of dance. Work is dance, death is dance, marriage is dance, birth is dance. I always wonder where we would be without dance. Now, power is dance. Unfortunately, the dancers are the women, gratefully singing praise to their 'husbands'.

It was like that in the old days, when rocks could move, when animals could talk and engage you in a serious argument about the ways of the world. Then, the women sang praise songs to their husbands returning from the hunt.

> Thank you, my fathers
> You who refused to die
> You the river that never dries
> The slippery fish hard to catch
> Only caught by the rich who can afford hooks
> You the river, meeting place of maidens.

That was one of the praise poems in the diet of my upbringing. The praise singer was my mother, my aunt, my niece, not my father or my uncle. Then, should I become head of state, what right have I to refuse to be worshipped, in song, dance, dress and ululations? Fortunately, I don't ever want to be head of state: politics is not my realm.

The Somali writer Nuruddin Farah once asked, 'How does it feel to see your face on the national coin? How does it feel to see your picture on all the dresses of the women of your country?'

Farah did not give an answer. I have no answer either. But I know I don't want to wear clothes with someone's picture unless they wear mine on theirs.

We have had ten years of women in our national politics, ten years of singing and dancing, ten years of ululations. Maybe the next ten years will also be ten years of real dance, for the heart and the emotions, this time by the men, in praise of woman. Or else women will remain of politics, not in politics.

As for me, I will remain silent, and sing to the raindrops that tickle my heart. I will sing the old songs of history and name my own heroes at the appropriate time, when they can no longer hear me, when they can no longer bend to the tune of flattery. But for now, I will be silent so that I can listen.

Never Mind, Sister,
This Is Our Home

My colleague, poet Musa Zimunya, once ended a poem with the line, 'Never mind, sister, this is our home.' Every time I go home, I can't resist feeling these words echoing again in my heart. 'Never mind,' I say to myself, 'this is my home where life is complex, simple, full of shadows and sometimes ghosts taking over life after dark.'

The last time I went home, mother had a headache. She sort of endures it quietly, with complaints only when over-questioned. 'One is bound to have some ailment,' she says. But I do not want her to leave it at that. I feel bad that she should have told me. But I also do not tell her that I feel bad since she will feel bad about my feeling bad and so would feel bad about telling me that she feels bad.

Meanwhile, the village huts threaten the sky with

their weak puffs of smoke nimbly wafting toward the heavens. 'You were born in one like this,' my mother reminds me. 'And there was no nurse with a white uniform,' she says. She knows that I have allowed other ways of seeing the world to invade my head. Way back she used to warn me that should I ever go to town, I must know that the ways of the city are like diarrhoea: they end.

'Mother, this is malaria country. If you do not come for treatment, it could be bad,' I warn her. She looks at me and does not bother herself with another remark, not even a question. 'This is malaria country,' she says, 'and when I gave birth to you, you did not refuse to come out because this is malaria country. I know you want me to come to the city. A terrible place to live. I want to visit and see my grandchildren, but to stay there, to be inside the fence all the time, like a goat that is waiting to be slaughtered, that is not easy for anyone to do,' she says.

Malaria country. Illiterate country. No roads. The narrow road that is there is the only one. The old bus that is there is the only one. One trip across mosquito country, across the land of no roads, the land full of cattle so thin that you can count their ribs from miles away.

But the faces that come to greet me are not full of anger. 'These are the people doomed to silence by this burden of illiteracy. To write in a country so burdened with illiteracy can be painful,' I cannot help saying to myself.

My uncle, the one with a wife pregnant for the

twelfth time, confronts me when I talk about reading. 'Your head is full of queer things,' he says. 'You want me at my age to sit side by side with my children at school, reading with these dying eyes of mine? What will come of the world?' He begins to read, letter by letter, following each word with his cracked fingers. 'We are farmers, you know. Not clerks who sit down all the time,' he says, his eyes pinned to the page of an old peasant farmers' guide.

I was born here. I grew up here. The soil under my feet harbours the very first blood that came out of me. The ears in this village heard the very first shrill cry that came out of my mouth. And they celebrated, with chickens, goats, sheep and pure white mealie-meal. The women ululated and the men left the home to drink in the comfort of a new arrival to their ranks.

Here too, the sun burns and my mother harbours a continuous headache. Everyone harbours a continuous something. And the roads are bad, no clinics nearby, no schools nearby — nothing. The only life that is here is the soil, rich black soil that gives so much life to the crops.

My brother looks at me and thinks I am already missing the city. 'You people surprise me. You come for a day, then think you are in hell. We live here and think we are in heaven. What sort of people are you?' he says, quaffing from the pot of traditional brew which he does not quite approve of. 'It might be good, but the alcohol ... Nobody ever knows how much alcohol there is in this thing.' He sips, winces and put the pot down, as if wondering whether he should continue this alcoholic war.

'You see,' my brother says, in a manner so philosophical everyone listens. He coughs, a rather shallow cough, dry at the end, but a cough anyway. 'You see. All these people, they live here. They don't envy any other world. A trip to Harare is like a trip to another country, in the jungle full of lions and jackals,' he says. 'Now you tell them you write books, they don't know what you are talking about. The only books they know are the books their children take to school. Or the old magazines which they have already used for rolling their cigarettes. Life is simple here. The only piece of paper they would not use for rolling a cigarette is the registration certificate. That is all. All else is simple and clear. If you want them to read, then buy them a beer, sit down and read them your stories,' he says.

I know that if the stories are boring, or badly read, they would walk out on me and I would wound myself. If the stories are good, they will buy some more beer until we are so drunk we cannot read anymore.

Then the talk shifts from the sexual exploits of the neighbour who has married his fourth wife, to light-hearted accusations of witchcraft.

At sunset, the women trek their long distances to the well, not with gourds on their heads this time but with five-gallon tins. And in the same old manner, the herd-boys bring the cattle home, with sheep and goats bleating their last choruses of the day. Soon the night will come, and the radio will take over the night which used to be the preserve of my mother thirty years ago when children swarmed around her to listen to her never-ending repertoire of folk tales.

Shebeen, Where People Drink

I have not been to a shebeen for many years, and I miss it. It is chaotic at the shebeen, where beer, women, fights and talk flow on loosely for as long as the boozers want.

I went, brushing aside the protests of both my wife and friends who insist on dwelling in the house of decency.

'Shebeens are illegal, you know,' they said. 'Yes,' I said, 'I know that very well. The police know it, and they drink there too,' I mocked. Everyone knows life begins at the shebeen, where people 'drink at home' and have the benefit of other services — shebeen talk and all that.

'The shebeen was born in Johannesburg,' says a beer fanatic, some sort of an expert on the history of shebeens. 'You see, it was during the last century when gold and diamonds bloomed and everyone went there. The wives of the miners probably had nothing much to do at the shanty where they waited for their husbands' return from work. So, they brewed and men came,' he says.

'Actually the people of Jo'burg did not invent the shebeen,' says a youngish woman wearing a mini-skirt short enough to reveal more than it covers. 'The people of Jo'burg just perfected it, like this German airline which did not invent flying but perfected it.' She laughs her rusty laughter, her voice full of dregs.

So, I add to myself, the women at the mines of Johannesburg must have taken to their traditional experience: why not brew some beer for these bored miners so that they can buy and meanwhile have some entertainment? So the men drank, got loose and loosened the women too. Many things happened.

'Excuse me, who is this man?' says a man, clean-shaven, rough-tongued but clear about his intentions. I had known it would come. The law of shebeens is: all strangers are either policemen or police informers. 'If he is a policeman, or some informer, let us know so that we can send him back to the police camp after giving him a pat on the head,' the man says. He stares at me with the eye of death, a knife dangling at his side.

The man who has brought me to the place looks at me, smiles to calm me down, and shouts, 'Hey, Gwature, calm down! He might have a beard like a detective, but do you think he would be a fool to come just like that? This is my in-law from another town. People from other towns must know that we have peaceful shebeens also,' my 'in-law' says. And for the first time I know I am an in-law to the man I had simply asked to take me and introduce me to a good 'sheb'.

I buy a few beers, one for me, one for the other most talkative guy with a beard like mine, one for the owner of the shebeen, a woman who has seen better days but who knows the interests of all generations.

'By the way, where were we?' says the other man, who seems to have had his story interrupted by our arrival. He scratches his head mischievously.

'Tell me if you should want some washdown for the beer,' my 'in-law' says, loudly, after taking a long sip of the beer I have bought him. And when the 'washdown' appears I look at the man in disbelief: the young girls of school-going age parade themselves as if to say, 'Which one of us?'

Everyone laughs. Their eyes point at me, in good humour. 'Thanks, but let us drink. Later, later,' I mumble. And the young girls leave, to the accompaniment of whistles and naughty humming. A few beers later I express my worry about AIDS. Everyone laughs at my foolishness. 'AIDS,' shouts the woman of the mini-skirt. 'Don't worry honey, we have condoms of steel if you prefer those.' Laughter fills the whole house, waking up the children in one of the rooms.

The woman owner stands up, leaves for a short while, comes back and says to one man, 'You can go.' As he walks into another room, mischievous eyes follow him. Later, he comes back with ruffled hair. 'How was it?' someone asks him teasingly.

But later shebeen talk spreads to other subjects. We would talk about the economy, about AIDS, about politicians, about everything, including the effects of alcohol on sexual behaviour.

'These politicians don't know what they are talking about most of the time,' says the shebeen historian. 'They want to ban the shebeen so that we will buy the white man's beer, making him richer and richer all the time. We have to take over the economy, and the first place is the shebeen.' Everyone agrees, in chorus.

'If they insist on fighting the shebeen to its death, I tell you they are throwing sand in their own political goulash,' says the woman who owns the place.

'She means it,' says my 'in-law'. 'She is a woman of influence. She knows every leader's girlfriend, name, address and age.' He nurses his beer with more confidence.

Then someone tells the story of how this same woman had an affair with a man, and when she thought he was going to leave her for a young one, she offered him her daughter. The man liked the young one but made a remark about old brooms knowing the corners of love. This to the joy of everyone, as the woman laughs too, unoffended.

'It's the hen which ate its own eggs,' remarks someone, casually.

'Never take offence at a shebeen,' a man says to me, the same one who had promised me a pat on the head if I were a police informer.

Meanwhile, beer flows on and those who have run out of money drink on and promise to pay at the end of the month. 'Don't worry, I will pay you, Mamoyo,' says the man with a beard like mine.

And later, as we stagger home, everyone talks of 'how nice a birthday party it was'. The woman owner announces that tomorrow is her dog's birthday, please come and enjoy life. So, it will be someone's or something's birthday for many years to come as the shebeen thrives on.

Harare's Sex Shops

There are no red-light districts in our sunshine city which, according to an advert, swims in the sun for fifteen hours a day. No red-light districts, no brothels, nothing, the city fathers will say, but ...

'The transport problem in this city is really bad,' says a stranger I have given a lift.

'What? I know we have a serious transport problem, but this is not the time to see it,' I caution the visitor, obviously a reader of some foreign newspaper which seems to emphasise the problems of our city as if there were nothing good about it.

To his amazement, I stop for a woman at the street corner. She opens the door and gets in, seating herself comfortably in the back seat.

'Where?' she says, gently, as if we have been intimate for a long time.

'What's your name?' I ask her, feigning naïvety about the ways of the city. 'Transport can become serious, especially when it's rather late, at the end of the month like this. Taxis take only long-distance customers, buses are over-loaded, emergency taxis are full before you know what is happening,' I sympathise with her.

I start the car and she looks frantic. 'Excuse me,' she interrupts me before I ask her where she wants me to drop her. 'Are you not from this city?'

When I say I am not from Harare, she is clear in her pronouncement: 'What makes you think that everyone who is by the roadside wants transport? The street corner is our shop-window, you see.' My friend is confused. He does not belong to these parts.

'I don't understand,' I say to her. I tell her I am driving to a friend's home and I thought she lived in the same area so I wouldn't mind giving her a lift.

'Lift?' she screams. 'Do you think I can eat a lift? Don't you guys like me? How can you treat me like a passenger like this?' I feel sorry for her and wonder what she would do if we were policemen who sometimes arrest women walking alone and lock them up for the night.

'Last night I was with a policeman, and he paid me well,' she says. 'Street corners are the sex shops of this city. You must know that,' she chides.

'Harare's sex shops,' I say to my friend as we abandon her, frustrated, wasting her time with a 'maybe tomorrow'.

Later in the Avenues, I drive slowly up the street to show my friend what has happened to our 'cleanest city in Africa'. Four women in mini-skirts and high heels do not come to the car. Instead they deliberately cross the road, wriggling their waists as they walk across the street in front of the car, unafraid.

We stop to greet them. 'I am Angela,' the older-looking one says, making up her face. 'Can I come in?' she requests. I say 'yes' and she gets in, beckoning her friend to join since she has just discovered there are two of us in the car.

'Twenty dollars for a brief moment at my place, forty dollars for the whole night,' she says. 'And I take good care of you, drinks included.' Once again we repeat the story of offering them a lift and all that nonsense. She laughs and gets out of the car, cursing.

As we drive round, we see many street corners with girls in mini-skirts, waiting but not waving down cars like those wanting to ask for a lift.

My friend is beginning to know the city and that it has sex shops just like those of some European cities. He thinks we must brave it and allow ourselves to be taken into one of the flats. Nothing wrong, I answer him, provided you are prepared to take the consequences.

Minutes later we are in a richly furnished flat, with the owner serving us whisky to the accompaniment of the jazz of our taste. She plays the latest sexy videos from Europe as part of her art of seduction.

'But my sister, where do you work?' I venture to ask her. 'I think I have seen you in some office,' I add. She looks at me with eyes that seem to say, 'This is not an office, though.'

'Yes, I work,' she says. 'I work and have a decent

job. This is a pastime, but AIDS is putting us out of it,' she complains. 'But we simply brush it aside. If a client is afraid of AIDS, we simply tell him that for the time being AIDS will be Acquired Immediate Desire for Sex,' she laughs.

Later she tells us that we look quite afraid of AIDS. She feels sorry for us, she says. So let us just drink and be friends. The woman is hospitable, refined and cheerful. 'I will never make love with condoms,' she later tells us. 'It's like eating a sweet covered in plastic,' she adds.

And when we leave, she asks us to come another day, to dance to music, to make friends. We could even bring our friends, male and female, to her place for a party in two weeks' time. We leave and go to a bar where single women sit and slowly sip their beer, dancing every now and then when the rhumba music compels them to.

Bars and street corners have become Harare's sex shops where men and women go to meet each other, to select and sometimes to fight over their choices. In the bars, a man who buys a woman a beer seems to be saying, 'I have selected you.' Or on the dance floor, a man who dances with her seems to say, 'I have selected you, but let's see your rhythm.'

Days later, when the new Minister of Health, Dr Timothy Stamps, reveals that the nation's population will decrease by nearly two million by the turn of the century, a friend bursts out, 'The guy should concentrate on finding the cure, not on threatening us with extinction.'

But meanwhile Harare's sex shops continue to thrive and funerals come and go. 'Since our women dress to kill,' says a friend, 'we are all going to die. The government should legislate against dressing to kill.' We laugh as we dance to the music of Thomas Mapfumo. He sings about a woman called Joyce:

Joyce, I will not let you go alone to your house today.

Joyce, I will not let you go alone today.

Queueing For Death

Imagine standing in a queue, waiting for your turn to die. Not in front of a firing squad. No. Not that. Zimbabweans are beginning to laugh about how they could very easily imagine themselves queuing for death in the hospital. It almost happened, three years ago, when coffins were in short supply and I could imagine that nurses were saying in their minds: people should queue up to die, one at a time.

'If queues could make people pregnant, all Zimbabweans, male and female, would be pregnant ten times over, with twins, triplets, quadruplets, quintuplets,' joked a man standing in a beer queue. He knew there were many other queues awaiting him, demanding, like the Shakespearean Shylock, their pound of energy.

If things or people are nicknamed according to their behaviour, then this city of sunshine could easily earn itself the title 'city of queues'. 'Soon, this town will be known as the town of swollen feet,' the beer-starved queuer laughs, his tobacco-laden teeth silently revealing their age in that sooty grin which suggests both anger and disquiet. The man, I thought, is part of Harare's streetscape, bored people standing in line for some service which never seems to come.

Harare is a city of nightmares, not nightmares of sleep, but queue nightmares and, recently, crime nightmares. Pickpockets and robbers have taken over pride of place in conversations.

Those who create queues seem to think that the absence of a queue is a sign of incompetence. And they are strict in ensuring that the queue be seen to be as long as it can be. Without queues outside their offices bureaucrats seem to think that they have no power. 'This is how we make small dictators,' a journalist friend once said as I was standing in a queue for press statements during a conference.

In the midst of African sweat and heat, the queues of Harare make life boring and irritating. I see queues in almost every street, every conceivable place, everywhere. I am sure that even in their sleep Harare's dreamers have weird nightmares of queues upon queues. Why not? The winding queues have become part of our minds, our emotions, our very language. The city's landscape is incomplete without people standing in long, winding queues.

For one reason or the other, Harareans will invent a queue at whatever cost and for whatever reason. At the entrance to a bank the clients sweat it out, waiting to withdraw a few dollars for their Christmas shopping.

In their hearts is also the pain of leaving the bank for the bus queue. But before they do that, they might be a little hungry, their stomachs rumbling. The little food kiosk at the corner demands that they wait in another queue for fifteen minutes or so.

Queues, queues, queues, from sunrise to sunset.

The other day, at the bank, the security man told me to stand outside the bank in a shapeless queue. The department in the bank I wanted to visit was full, he said. I stared at him. He looked me direct in the face as if his eyeballs had teeth to chew me up. 'Stand outside until I call you to come in,' he shouted. I refuse to be intimidated by his dull green uniform which is a distant relative of army camouflage. Of course he does not wield a gun but instead a heavy, strong staff, the flat-headed knobkerrie, as they call it in these parts. I insist that there is no way I will go and stand outside in a never-ending queue. 'Can I see so-and-so in the bank? Phone him and tell him I am around, waiting to see him,' I say to the man.

He picks up the phone and feigns dialling. I remind him that was not the way to dial an internal number. He threatens me with all sorts of faces and words, including expulsion from the place if I do not behave myself. In the end, he allows me in, grudgingly, mumbling something about me being a 'chef', an important person. Yes, it is only those who do not know anybody who stand in the queues, worn out, despised as if their time did not matter a hoot.

No wonder that a Zimbabwean musician has been satirising the security guards in one of his popular tunes, 'Mahobo':

> Please, please, please,
> Mahobo, let me in,
> I am not here to see you.
> I am here to see the manager,

the singer wails after the security man has become an impassable wall.

Where in Harare, Bulawayo and other cities will I be served without undergoing the queue endurance test? I want a box of matches costing three cents, the queue for it detains me for thirty minutes. I want to buy a good loaf of bread for sixty cents, the queue for it will steal me from work for another thirty minutes.

But what is thirty minutes compared to the three or four hours that bus commuters spend in the queue? Imagine leaving work at five o'clock in the evening, joining a queue fifteen minutes later and waiting there for two hours. The first bus which comes has bad news: not your bus. The second is half-full when it stops. The third is already full and it comes simply as a formality. So I say: okay, I will go to the pirate taxis.

The same story begins all over again. The queues are so long and rough that I decide to go back to the buses. I know it is about to rain and I do not have an umbrella to shield myself. I do not mind the risk. Worse things have happened to me. Bus accidents and all that, with tyre bursts to make the whole thing dramatic. For such is the drama of existence in Harare with its queues.

When the downpour starts, I am already half-way in the queue but I have to abandon it, giving way to those who either have umbrellas or have developed a certain immunity to heavy rain and the intimidating flashes of lightning. I leave and go to the pub, waiting for the rains to subside. The author of *Waiting for the Rain*, Charles Mungoshi, is there too, waiting for the rain to subside. But we both know it is the queues which we want to subside, in this city of sunshine, in the land of progress.

Sorry Madam,
No Offence Intended

The soothing music from the quiet bars of Harare's hotels is usually irresistible. Any passer-by who feels compelled to enter learns a few cultural lessons: no jeans, no shorts, no T-shirts, sometimes no un-accompanied ladies. Yes, that is what a Nigerian friend discovered when the jacket-and-tie rule was forcibly applied to him wearing his happy, flowing gowns of rich Nigerian cloth.

Being reasonably well-travelled myself, I have concluded that one of the surest ways of measuring society's basic attitudes towards myriad issues is through hotel service, especially in matters of gender.

One day a lady friend took me out to lunch, insisting that she would rather do away with the male prerogative of asking ladies out for meals.

Why not the other way round, she argued. I

yielded, and soon we dissuaded ourselves from the never-ending routine of scheduled meetings and work. We walked into our chosen hotel, asked for a table and were soon happy to be seated. After having the usual version of beef and something, plus drinks, the lady asked for our bill.

The waiter coolly handed over the bill to me. I was not quite broke, but the good lady was, indeed, taking me for lunch. My budget would not allow me to volunteer either. My lady colleague was as much disappointed as I was curious to find out the meaning of the waiter's behaviour. 'Excuse me,' I said, 'couldn't you have given the lady the bill since she is the one who asked for it?' The waiter looked at me, dumbfounded, his eyes visibly horrified at what sort of a man I was, as if those dark eyes were trying to fathom the depth of my stupidity and lack of culture. 'You know,' he stammered, coughing a little bit before going on. 'The bill is always given to the man. It is the man who takes the woman out,' he sealed the conversation, to the utter disgust of my female colleague. His face read that, as far as he was concerned, she was not an important subject of discussion. Although the lady paid the bill, it was not before she had exchanged a few sharp words with the manager, warning him that certain attitudes served with the local menu in the hotel were not useful for the progress of the female section of our society. But I knew she was up against a huge flood of overt and covert attitudes embedded in the man.

Then the other day I went to have a drink with

friends, male and female. The bills always came to the men even when the women journalists had placed the orders. The women simply looked on at it all, resigned after many purposeless protests. 'Let me do the job the way I have been trained to do it,' one waiter reminded a female colleague.

As far as waiters in Harare are concerned, the female is still an economic minor even if she may be a 'boss' at her workplace. Imagine a woman managing director taking a junior manager out to lunch and ending up with the anti-climax of the bill being handed to her junior. While it may boost the male ego of the junior manager, I am sure it burns coals of anger in the female managing director.

Three years ago I gave one of my relatives a jolt when he visited me in the office. I was working for a publishing house at the time. A woman rushed into my office, demanded to see a few editorial reports I had made and went out again, whereupon my relative asked me how it was that I could allow my secretary to bully me like that. Horror came to his face when I told him that the lady was my boss.

Of course, the average Zimbabwean woman is economically frail due to the educational imbalances created by a history of colonialism in which a woman was not expected to work. The Rhodesian white 'medem' felt insulted and humiliated if she had to work, and it was a sign of economic desperation if she had to work alongside her husband. This attitude spread across to black Rhodesians, even though the government exempted women from paying the notorious head tax.

'These waiters are members of the old guard. They will have to be replaced by young people who are receptive to change,' a female journalist once said. But she was again frustrated when a young waiter, barely two years in the job, presented all the bills to the men around.

Ever since I started observing these social deformities, I have made efforts to draw waiters' attention to the problem. All the time I end up with the feeling that some underlying force is behind the failure of the many feminists trying to correct these attitudes. My fear has always been the realisation that the old Rhodesian 'medem' is still very much alive in our land, being taken out, not working, feeling insulted if presented with the bills and insisting on being called 'medem' while her husband is the usual unknighted 'sah' of the old Rhodesian tales. The Rhodesian 'sah' is alive and around, in his khaki shorts, with his bushy beard and a face worn out from farming the land.

Old attitudes are harder to destroy than love. Rhodesians, both black and white, never die, so the song went on at independence. And so the black Zimbabwean woman is sad if she does not have a maid to order around in the home while she sits and watches television. Of course, the maid is in full uniformed paraphernalia in the old Rhodesian manner, wearing a cap and with 'a reasonable command of English'.

A Walk Through Harare's Sanitary Lane

A man — or is it a woman? — creeps up to the dustbin, fumbles inside it with long hands, rough and torn. I stop the guessing game of 'man' or 'woman' and simply accept 'person' as a more durable substitute. Plop, a large cat jumps out of the dustbin, mewing, escaping, refusing to be denied breath and comfort, clinging to life, escaping death. Another person in torn rags walks by, barefoot, uttering words which no unaccustomed ear could discern. The other mumbles something, as if to say, yes, do not worry, those are the ways of the world. No need for argument.

The scene, an alleyway, is the meeting place for beggars, cats, stray dogs and street children. There language is fresh, not quite insulting, not quite respectful, not so dignified. The expression, too, is not quite so welcoming and I feel an intruder, an uninvited guest, maybe with the stink of a corpse. Who said an uninvited guest and a corpse soon stink? I cannot remember, but I feel like both.

The time? After five when the workers of the city scramble to leave, to go home to their townships or their posh suburbs where a stray dog prompts an announcement over the radio or a child loitering at the gate causes serious legal debate on the abuse of children. Not here, in the alleyway. No radio announcements, no legal wrangles, no lights. The only wrangles here are the struggle between dog and man, between death and life.

The alleyway is not a thing of the past. The real Harare is a city of alleyways. For every bright street, lit day and night, colourful with flowers and artificial trees, there is, right behind, in the shadows, the alleyway, the byway which seems immune from municipal by-laws, tucked away like the shadow of a dead man. The alleyway, or sanitary lane, as the poet Musa Zimunya calls it, lurks behind all the Christmas niceties like a shadow.

The alleyway has its clothes — old, discarded newspapers, torn gumboots, rain-drenched, discarded old tins threatening to cut the bare soles of cracked feet, old blankets where lice and dust embrace. I see all this, in the middle of the glitter and glow of the city, and feel hurt. This is the sanitary lane, the place of many dialogues, a place where gesture encounters gesture, the groan of death mingles freely with the rumble of a starved stomach.

'What do girls eat?' says a young boy, aged anything below ten, but wise in the ways of Harare's sanitary lanes. 'Ice cream,' the other boys chorus back, naming that special treat which many boys in this city centre of ice-cream trolleys and adverts know is a rare gift with which young girls could be trapped into love. I look at the young faces and hear their silent words of pain, of the capacity to endure, telling me the story of my intrusion and its consequences.

The boys from the sanitary lane are the boys who guard cars during the day, for no fixed price. They run around the thief-infested parking areas, offering to 'keep the car' for whatever the vehicles' owners can offer. Sometimes the police get annoyed, especially when tourists write letters to the newspapers complaining of being molested. Police swarm into the streets, conducting a wild chase which forces the boys off the streets, just for a day or two. When they come back their faces are more determined, with new recruits and new skills for evading the stiff-necked police.

The sanitary lane remains nameless, 'of no fixed abode', the police say when they arrest the street children for 'vagrancy'.

But in today's only daily, there is the picture of the President, flanked by his Minister of Finance, Economic Planning and Development. The minister has announced his Economic Reform Programme in language which no one can either understand or eat. The more he says the economy has grown, the more the beggars look desperate, worn out, with fewer coins in their plates and more misery-laden songs.

I walk through the sanitary lane, thinking about Christmas, how the beer will flood the throats of the guzzlers, how some will die of over-eating and the healthy blood which will flow on the roads. This is not healthy blood, I think to myself, looking at the skins worn on the faces of the inhabitants of the sanitary lane.

Thinking about Christmas is as interesting as it is annoying. Way back in those days of rain and plenty, I mean the sixties, the days when they used to bake buns which smelled like real buns, the days when bread from the city made us salivate, those were the days when Christmas was Christmas. Musa Zimunya paid tribute in verse to those memories. But this is annoying, to think of Christmas and dull cakes, in the sanitary lane, the place with no fixed address.

Then the city came in full swing, with it alleyways, the narrow streets which no one seems to see, no one seems to care about. They are there all the time, reminding the city's inhabitants that the world is not as bright as the many other colours of the rainbow splashed on the city's tall buildings, those outbursts of cream, red and white. The alleyways are dark, personal, full and threateningly meditative.

Next time I visit the alleyway, the sanitary lane, I know what I will hear. The old dialogue between fly and baby continues, with song and tears to the accompaniment of rusty, resigned laughter of the discarded woman and man, those who know only the colour of scars and the smell of unbandaged wounds.

Witches, Ghosts and Others

I have often wondered how urban people, I mean the urbanised, those who left home a long time ago, handle problems. They have earned themselves a new name in Zimbabwe's cities, especially amongst those are born and bred in the cities, the dark parts, the semi-lit and those fully aglow with city lights. In Harare, they call them '*bhonorokishini*' (born-in-locations). See what the English language can endure when people corrupt it and bend it for their own convenience.

The other day I went to see my sister in one of the oldest locations of Harare. She was as forthcoming as usual, unburying her meagre earnings from her tomato and vegetable stalls to send a boy dashing to buy me *chibuku*, my favourite brew. The boy did not take long before rushing back, breathless, speechless.

'What is the problem?' my sister asked the empty-handed boy. But before he could speak, we all rushed out in the manner of people jumping out of an overturned bus. We heard screams from the other end of the street; already crowds had gathered, standing by, shouting for the police, for anyone with first-aid skills but doing nothing to assist.

The incident: a young boy of sixteen was lying on the hard ground. Someone had stabbed him in the back and in the chest. Steaming red blood was gushing out of him, draining him of life. His faint cries told the story of death, the agony. The boy was almost dead. That is a street fight the Hararean way, in the dark 'high-density' suburbs where people look crime in the face and are too tired or bored to rush and call the police.

Everyone was asking what had happened, more interested in the story than in the dying youth. Everyone had their own story, narrated from the heart, with thrills of how they themselves could have been involved in the scuffle. How close it was. How terrible the police are to remain inactive in the face of of all this crime. How terrible.

But they were all for the story rather than the victim. Then I realised that in an accident the story attracts more attention than the victim. In an accident the stories improvised for the occasion need first aid. Every onlooker has his own story, well brewed and sustained to believable proportions.

'You must consult a medicine-man,' a woman shouts from among the crowd to one of the relatives who has come to the spot. 'How could it happen to my own son, not any of the other sons of other people?' she asks, insistent that the world needs more medicine-men than there are around.

On the faces of the crowd, the idea of more medicine-men seems plausible, a normal way to conduct things. And I wonder how many city-dwellers consult medicine-men in times of crisis.

A friend who works for the Ministry of Political Affairs comes to my rescue two days later as we visit my sister. We see one of the relatives of the dead boy collecting even the tiny bits of sand where blood had dropped. The woman is painstakingly picking up every bit, including little blades of grass, until she ends up scratching parts of the blood-stained security wall, taking the dust away with her. Saying silent words to the dead, to herself, in some gesture of magical-spiritual significance.

'You should know what she will do with all those bits and pieces. It is like election time,' he says. 'When election time comes, medicine-men in this country take money. Even the big politicians consult them in the midst of the night,' the man laughs, remembering that his task is to locate good and exclusive medicine-men for the chefs — important people — so that they can get the best advice and divination about the death or life of their political careers.

A story is told of how a politician found a good medicine-man, consulted him successfully and then bought a house in the city for the good man of herbs to be kept under guard so that other politicians could not visit him. When later, in another election, the same politician's fortunes died, the man of power expelled the man of herbs and refused to pay him.

And whenever I talk about death by natural causes, my old aunt refuses to hear of it. Even at her late age, over 90 years old, she thinks some witch would have to envy the prospect of the taste of her flesh. So when she dies, the witch, using her magical powers, would extract the old bones from the grave and use them somehow. Even when the seed in her dry fields does not germinate and the neighbours' germinates, she is not slow to identify the game witches play in such cases. Even the rain is subject to the power of witches and weird medicine-men.

I was content that superstition is a burden of so-called 'underdevelopment', but the other day I talked to a writer in Europe. We walked as we talked and he was quick to point out a 'haunted house' to me. Inside me, I was also quick to realise how we have kept the old order, the different way of arranging the world, as a journalist friend once said. He was commenting about ghosts, witches and magic, the way those forces work with a different logic in every society, the way they have been marginalised simply because they operate secretly.

When next someone speaks to me about witches, ghosts and so on, I expect to see them anywhere, in the city and in the village where my mother lives under constant threats from 'witches' and their unknowable powers which can be set loose by the slightest provocation.

A Dance of Graduates and Illiterates

June or July of every year, not just this one, comes and goes and the city is veiled with black gowns. A Harare of flowing black robes, students graduating in the manner of monks of the yesteryear of European civilisation. And speeches too about manpower provision, the supply of skills to industry and commerce, to everywhere that skills are needed.

And I am part of it too, in the midst of this young life full of hope and careers and professions. For recently I have been honoured by the National University, my own university, fond memories of which I hold in the depths of my heart. I have been appointed to the honorary chair of writer-in-residence, and everyone wonders what my duties are. And I wonder too, since it is a non-teaching post and students have no idea what to call me, lecturer or writer.

I smile as I sit in this biggish, rather profusely pretentious office where the walls are polished pure white every day and the table and chairs are oiled shiny every two days. This is my first office appointment in four years, during which time I have been some sort of wanderer 'of no fixed abode'.

'I came here to write books,' has been my verbal defence as students, shy and unsure, invade my office, humbly asking for wise guidance in the writing of poems, novels, plays, anything, including love letters. Students always have a knack for believing that even their amorous missives have great literary merit. Yes, they flood my office, their faces full of a future they cannot know, their eyes bright as the new moon out there, or the city lights which flash hope into the rural unemployed until they come to seek work in the city of golden dreams.

And I see it all, smiling inside my heart, that the world looks good for this young blood. 'No baby must cry,' I recall the line from a poet friend – and no tears must ever flow off their faces, I add. They are here at this institution of hope so that they can remove the burden of unemployment from their minds.

But deep down, I harbour fear, a persistent fear which, like an ominous shadow, refuses to abandon me. There is the smell of the Structural Adjustment Programme in the wind, with its flags swamping those of political independence. 'Sure Advice to Poverty' local pub humorists have nicknamed this World Bank-IMF economic beverage. It tastes sour from the beginning, a cartoonist once wrote as he watched friends and foes losing jobs in Harare's industries under the banner of 'die today so as to live tomorrow'.

Then in the afternoon I give a lift to a young woman, charming and youthful, with beauty and simple grace. 'Coming to graduate, I suppose?' I start the conversation, trying to say at least something in the depth of the silence of strangers. My old Datsun rattles on (may the Japanese be forgiven). The young woman looks at me, stealing a full glance, with a hint of recognition on her face, then withdraws into the realm of silence. She still has some reservations, but as her voice breaks out, confidence too arrives. As she answers a gentle yes to my old question, it is subdued, burdened with rocks and dark clouds of the unknown worries in her heart.

I wonder, in the silence, why such a young woman, graduating, should be so burdened, hopeless on a day which must surely beat even her birthday. We speak on, in broken sentences, exploring our experiences, our stories. I am a writer, she says of me. 'And you are a former student,' I giggle. 'Now I am a job-seeker,' she jokes too, her face brighter than before, eyes glittering in that captivating manner of the innocent and inexperienced. And when I say 'jobs' she looks at me, her eyes alive.

'Jobs, jobs, jobs, and graduates too: 2,000 new ones have been capped, and they join the nearly 200,000 secondary-school-leavers who lie on the lawns every day, waiting for jobs. Those who wait by the gates of the city's industrial sites, dreaming that one day a personnel manager will point his finger in their direction and offer them a job. This is a dream which some have kept alive for over ten years as the job-seekers' figures swell every year-end. Examination rooms churn them out in their hundreds, fully-equipped with the magic of five O levels.'

'I have an honours degree in industrial psychology,' the youthful woman says to me, 'but I have been looking for a job for the past eight months. They know me at all the employment agencies. At every company in town they have well-typed letters from me. But I discovered one thing: you have to know someone for you to get a job,' she says gently. This time her voice is sad, pained and hurt. And as I drop her near Harare's Central Park, her words echo in my mind alongside the voices of the many unemployed, those always on hand to partake of any free entertainment in Harare's First Street. Never mind the nature of the entertainment, be it a fight or an improvised dance by beggars, the crowds continue to swell.

Meanwhile, graduation gowns and parties drown the city in their black, gold, green and yellow, showing the endangered hierarchies of knowledge. Speeches have flooded the papers, promises have burst the seams of the imagination of secondary-school children as they watched on television or listened to the radio.

'We have entered a new dance, a dance of graduates and illiterates, unemployment,' the voice of a friend echoes in my mind. The words refuse to die in my mind, in the mind of this city where the sun does not shine for the unemployed. And I sit in the university chair, learning to invent new dreams for those who already have invented old ones which are now shattered.

The City of Problems
and Laughter

'When times are hard, we survive by way of laughter,' goes a common belief in the city, remarking on the humour of Harare, where everything turns to laughter, even death. The humour of the place runs deep, through every vein of life.

In the pubs a story circulated of a Zimbabwean politician who committed suicide by taking a pesticide. When he got to heaven, God asked people to stand in groups according to their professions and class while they were on earth. The politician joined those of his class but God was annoyed. 'Hey you, why do you want to cheat? You were a farmer, not a politician. Even the smell of the pesticide does not work to remind you of your profession,' the good God chided to the amusement of St Peter and all the others at court.

Harareans dismiss the AIDS virus and the threat it poses with the contempt of new graffiti on bus-stop shelters and other public places: 'AIDS: American Idea for Discouraging Sex'.

When recently the Zimbabwean government yielded to the Structural Adjustment Programme of the IMF and the World Bank, the humour-makers simply called for a Sexual Adjustment Programme to be introduced to run alongside the Structural Adjustment Programme.

Then someone had an idea. A radical economist had argued that the IMF's Structural Adjustment Programme was going to cause much suffering, especially children dying of malnutrition. The humour-makers did not run short of ideas. 'Down with the Infant Mortality Fund' read a slogan on one of the dirty walls of a township close to the city.

Even the preachers take it upon themselves to pray for the economy. 'God, we the poor are no longer like Lazarus. Our rich people are worse. They throw the crumbs so far away that we can't find them,' a poet-preacher prayed, to the amazement of all.

Zimbabwe has a good neighbourliness policy, but unfortunately one neighbouring state, Zambia, seems to be the source of one of the most obnoxious national problems: game poaching. Zambians sneak across the border, armed to the teeth, and invade one of the most beautiful wild game reserves in the world. The illegal hunters are called poachers and they die in battle as Zimbabweans track them down in the park.

'You Zimbabweans are funny also,' says a local

humour-maker. 'When I am in Zambia, I am a professional hunter. But when I cross the border, you call me a poacher.' The man argues that every man is a poacher. 'Depends on what you poach,' he says. 'As for me, I poach on street corners and in the pubs, here in the city.' He looks at a woman sitting next to him; quite drunk she is, but he does not mind. 'I poach an animal and the animal eats unfamiliar grass. What do I do?' he excuses himself, calls a taxi and silently sends her home. 'I will have to start poaching again,' he sighs.

And there is a children's teaser about an ugly politician who also happens to be a minister. Harareans will ask each other in mock-drama fashion: what crime is it to kill the president? 'Murder,' they say. And killing the Minister of Finance? 'Tax-murder,' they say. And this ugly minister? 'Oh, I will be charged with poaching.'

When there is too much news about ministers, television viewers at home or newspaper readers on the bus will make a remark, to nobody in particular — 'This newspaper, always news about the monster of health, or the monster of education. When will we, the ordinary citizens, get into the news?' and the woman on the next seat chips in, 'When you eat glass.'

Shebeen patrons were quick to remark on the recent spurt of price increases, 'The price of beer goes up, the price of mealie-meal goes up, the only thing which doesn't go up is my salary.' But another guy reminds him that salaries have been increased recently. 'Forget it,' the protester quips, 'my salary walks up on the steps while prices go up with the escalator.'

As the unemployment problem causes havoc in the cities, the youth themselves are the first to create stories about it. One youth told me he had an idea which he wants to try. 'They always ask us for five O level subjects as if those subjects can work. But I will fix them. Me and four others with one O level subject each are going to form a co-operative. We will take our certificates and turn up for a job,' he laughs.

When the police get involved in criminal activities, Harareans take it in their stride. 'This is like sending a fly to a milk jar,' they remark before twisting the Criminal Investigation Department to read 'Criminals' Information Department'.

Harareans, they laugh at everything, even Members of Parliament who are shown on television taking a snooze in the House of Assembly. 'They should just call it the house of dreams,' says a tax-payer as he sees his money being spent worthlessly. 'In Europe there would be an angry demonstration against lazy Members of Parliament.'

When the chips were down and there was so much theft in the city, the public, who are usually more informed than the police, claimed there was an association of thieves. Before long it had even a name, ZATO. Short for Zimbabwe African Thieves' Organisation.

'There is no such thing,' a senior police officer said the other day. 'It is not registered,' he said. 'The police are something else,' a beer guzzler was not slow in arguing back. 'What does he expect them to register as, a welfare organisation or a business venture?'

So they laugh on as they face life. They will call women 'those with Fanta faces and Coca Cola legs' if they over-use make-up, or call big-bellied politicians 'those of the Rhodesia front', or even go so far as to call one bank the 'Bank of Crooks and Criminals'. Or worse still, tell stories of a soccer referee who showed a red card to his wife's lover when he found the lover had intruded into the soccer man's own bedroom.

Daring Harareans, there is nothing they will not do to survive: the other day a thief poured dried hot pepper into the eyes of a security guard who was on his way to the bank to deposit a few thousand dollars, and Harareans now say the man was charged with 'culpable peppercide'.

Cleaning the Streets
for the Queen

When it comes to sweeping, there are different ways of doing the job, especially in Harare. It is eleven years now since independence and the cities of the country have discovered a new manner of holding the broom. Yes, the broom.

'You are an African. When a visitor comes to your place, do you not sweep the yard?' a friend reported an amiable conversation he had recently had with the mayor of Harare. The mayor knows about sweeping and, with the assistance of the town clerk, he does indeed sweep.

Mbare, Harare's oldest suburb, is the target for this year's sweeping. There have been brooms seen there on several occasions, the ones they sell on the market. But, no, do not think of those. There are brooms that sweep other types of dirt.

Whenever I walk in Mbare I look around and recall the pictures of Soweto on television, with the South African police and army bulldozing the illegal settlers. Talk of brutality, there it is. I understand that some Sowetan women even stripped naked in front of the oncoming bulldozers but soon realised that they would be buried naked. They ran for their lives. Life is too short and rough to waste it.

Harareans seem to have learnt their experience from the South Africans. I suspected it would happen. I mean the sweeping, not the learning.

Come October this year, the big Commonwealth Conference will be held in the Zimbabwean capital. 'Heads of State Jet In' is likely to be a semi-permanent headline in the local daily. Then sub-editors will have to rest a bit in the couple of days after the heads of state and government from all over the Commonwealth have landed at Harare International Airport.

But then there is a small snag. The Queen of England, yes, the Queen herself, has requested to visit one of the most run-down suburbs of Harare, Mbare. Now, there is a problem: who can stand up and say to Her Majesty, 'No, Your Majesty, please go to the other places, Borrowdale, Greendale, not the squatter-riddled Mbare.' Mbare is chaotically planned and everything takes care of itself. Violence, drugs, illegal vendors selling anything you can imagine. And collapsing buildings, old ones built in nineteen-I-don't-know-when.

A broom is a remarkable invention. Praise be to the inventors. The dirt in the house leaves as soon as a broom enters.

Harare city council has a new broom, the law. The mayor was not talking of sweeping away real dirt. He was talking of the squatters settled in the Mbare area because of Harare's acute shortage of housing. The mayor's broom sweeps human beings, dumping them into some sort of rubbish pit so that the Queen does not see them.

It is a matter of public relations. The Queen of England must go away with a 'favourable' impression. I don't know what that means. But I do know that it has to do with pretence, appearances, appearances. What I know about appearances is that when I was at school the motto on our school badge was 'Be, rather than appear to be'. The canon is 'Thou shalt not pretend'.

Meanwhile, the squatters, their little children in Mbare, will wonder what the Commonwealth Conference is all about when they have to be dumped on society's rubbish heap. Where that is, no one knows. Thank God, and the ancestors too, the season is neither cold nor rainy.

I wonder what is so special about the Queen that the lives of simple people can be turned upside-down in such a short time. In her own country, to which I have been on many occasions, there are squatters and homeless people. I have never seen them being 'cleaned away' when she passes by. They are a sore part of British life, but at least they are allowed to exist. Here they are 'cleaned away' as if they could just be imagined away and forgotten. The wretched of the earth whose cries and moans power hates to hear.

This is not the first time Harareans have felt the sweeping power of the law's broom. When the non-aligned meeting came in 1986 there was a vicious sweeping of the streets of Harare. Women walking alone were presumed to be soliciting for men, the rich delegates to the conference. They were picked up, locked in some far-away cells and released later. A few married women fell into the angry hands of the police and today the scars of the occasion still linger in their minds. I saw it with my own eyes and a few years later I wrote a radio play on the subject, *Sister, Sing Again Some Day.*

Then it happened again when the Pope came over for a couple of days. A not-so-holy broom preceded him, sweeping human beings under the holy carpet. May their souls rest in their woven dreams. And the holy man went away thinking: how holy this place looks, so clean. That is, if physical cleanliness can measure spiritual cleanliness.

As I write, I have just heard the news that yesterday a high court judge dismissed the town clerk's appeal to evict the squatters. 'In any case, perhaps the applicant, the city of Harare, and others who are so anxious to sweep the respondents [the squatters] under the red carpet to be rolled out for Her Majesty's visit to Mbare need to be reminded that the liberation war in Zimbabwe was fought primarily over the issue of land, combined with the goal of justice for all,' ruled Mr Robinson, the wise judge.

I always wonder whether we have ever stopped eating from the fruit of amnesia, forgetting that the squatters we see all over the place in our cities remind us of our lost objectives. Someone wrote a book, *Zimbabwe: A Revolution That Lost Its Way*. I don't blame him. For we have now opted for full-time economic structural adjustment whose simple principle is: he who has a bigger purse has a bigger say. Forget about human rights, the right to a home, the right to life, the right to human treatment, the right to a decent meal. These rights are not written about in the law books.

I am alone now, walking down Second Street, passing near parliament, the house of empty promises, to the national newspaper, the media of omissions. I hear disgruntled voices, some speak of economic stomach adjustment, some talk humorously of 'when independence will come to an end', others lie on the tired park benches hoping for a decent meal, but the squatters will have to dream of no fixed abode for a while, until the Queen of England shakes their invisible hands and says 'goodbye to Zimbabwe' in her bird of metal.

Vendors, Policemen and Death

A policeman chases a young boy along busy First Street, a vendor selling vegetables and fruit in the middle of the city. His boots thud as he screams, panting for breath. Pedestrians in the streets of Harare look on amazed. In their eyes are so many questions, unasked questions, burning ones, sad questions. I am part of the crowd, as usual.

'This is Harare,' a bystander says to no one in particular, to himself. 'This is Harare where it is a crime to sell healthy and fresh vegetables and fruit.' The man walks away. He has no more words. And I think about it all: they are 'cleaning' the city for the October Commonwealth summit.

Meanwhile, the policeman has grabbed the seven-teen-year-old boy and slaps him hard on the face after grabbing the vegetables and fruit from him. A saddened crowd of Harareans looks on, eyes gaping, some remarking, others feeling betrayed.

Someone stands up to the policeman. 'This boy is trying to earn an honest living and you beat him up as if he has committed a crime,' shouts the man. The crowd agrees with the bold man. They scream at the policeman to leave the boy alone. 'Leave him alone to earn an honest living. What do you want him to do? You want him to steal? Go and arrest the pickpockets who haunt us all the time in the streets of the city.' I hear their voices, desperate voices full of anger and pain in this city where you need a licence to do everything, anything.

Pressure and anger build up. The crowd threatens to mob the policeman if he continues. The air is tense. The crowd moves in on the policeman. Fear reigns in the eyes of the man in uniform. He leaves the boy alone. But before long another policeman, more senior and with more medals, arrives. He quickly senses what is happening, handcuffs the boy and drags the screaming youth away to the police station.

Power and powerlessness, I think to myself. The boy would not be able to afford the spot fine. So he has already spent a day in the cells. His crime: selling vegetables and fruits in the streets without a licence. And when he comes out of that cell, his fresh vegetables and fruits will have been confiscated. He will be hungry. His parents will be angry with him for exposing himself to the police before selling enough to support the family. And the boy will not know what is good or bad. So he might even think of committing other more serious crimes, robbing a passenger at the bus terminus or something.

For many years I have watched and wondered at the brutalisation of Zimbabwean society. The other day I was talking to a fellow writer who had escaped death by inches. After taking the local taxi home, he had given the driver the fare, a five-dollar note, but the driver mistook it for a two-dollar note. An argument ensued. The man brought out a long knife and demanded more money. Fortunately the writer had matches which he lit for the driver to show him that it was just a misunderstanding.

'Our society is so brutalised,' the writer still shakes his head, remembering how he could easily have been stabbed with a sharp knife, killed for a mere three dollars. 'Why did the driver not think of calling the police or something?' my friend wonders.

Life, death, so cheap. Even as I write this story, bus-drivers and owners are up in arms against the government for introducing new and tighter regulations against those who drive under the influence or those who allow themselves to drive defective buses on the roads.

'Malicious regulations,' the drivers and bus-owners have said. This is despite the fact that two weeks ago a drunken bus-driver killed 89 school children who had been out on a happy sporting day. While the children played, he drank his usual heavy dose of alcohol. On the way back, despite protests from teachers and pupils, he drove too fast and the bus overturned, killed nearly all the teenagers in the bus and a few of the teachers accompanying them.

At the central bus terminal, the vibrant centre

where long-distance buses converge from all corners of the Zimbabwean earth, the drivers and bus-conductors shove and push. They employ pushers, in the Japanese manner, who shove passengers to get them in place like goats being packed for slaughter.

In a bus with a capacity of 75, they do not hesitate to load over 125 near-suffocating passengers. Because of Zimbabwe's transport blues, passengers cannot afford to protest.

'Buy your own bus if you want to travel like a king,' the conductor says. So, the passengers murmur and only look. 'When will we reach this journey's end?' I recall the lines I once wrote when I took the long-distance bus. The police had stopped the driver and checked the tyres. The man of law called the conductor outside and queried him about the condition of one of the front tyres. I sat by the window, looking at the pair, my window open and my ears awake. The man of law was not happy with the condition of one of the tyres and he said so.

'We are people of the same blood,' the conductor pleaded, shoving a five-dollar note into the police-man's expectant fingers. My heart nearly collapsed inside me. A five-dollar note changed hands and we could all die.

Ten minutes later we had an accident: the same tyre had burst and death stared us in the face like a murderer, over 100 passengers dying for the sake of a five-dollar note. Luckily we survived with just a few bruises and no apology from the driver or conductor. The journey was resumed three hours later after sticking on another worn-out tyre which punctured 100 kilometres further on.

'Economic corruption that puts no value to human life,' I say to myself. This is like the land of dreams where a life is measured in small coins.

'This is how we brutalise our own people,' I said to a fellow writer days later as I recounted the story. A sad story of how those who travel by bus live every day. As for me, farewell to the brutalisation of the people, the honest citizens living precarious lives under roofs of plastic paper, and death under the blade of rickety buses and emergency taxis.

Marengenya:
Tipsy, Dead Drunk, or Having a Head

'At lunch they drink beer, after work they drink beer, then they stagger home to snore heavily before waking up gripped by a vicious hangover,' a friend of mine said of the leisure pursuits of my fellow Zimbabweans, especially the men. Then the whole thing starts all over again, in an attempt to quell the hangover. 'Avoid a hangover, stay drunk,' says a local car-sticker.

There is a story of a father who always made sure he came home drunk, smelling heavily of alcohol. His little son always smelt the beer until he began to think it was his daddy's peculiar perfume. Then one day the small boy passed a beerhall from which the heavy stench of the traditional brew punched his nose. 'Mummy, I can smell Daddy here,' the innocent one observed.

'Zimbabwean blacks don't know how beautiful their country is,' the chairman of the tourism board once mourned. This ageing man is employed to ensure that Zimbabweans, blacks especially, admire the beauty of their country. The hope was that in the end they would, instead of going 'home' (*kumusha*), visit the tourist resorts, abandoning the visits home which are reminiscent of the era of white rule before 1980. Then blacks knew beyond doubt that they came to the city to provide labour for the white man's industry and travelled back to their rural homes to relax and be human beings once more.

The old gentleman simply cannot appreciate that the African sense of leisure may not coincide with the European sense of the joys of life. It is also a matter of aesthetic differences. Never mind the magical waters of the *Musi Wa Tunya* (The Smoke That Thunders) — Victoria Falls — as they roar and thunder to excite the most sleepy imagination. Never mind the wonders of the Great Zimbabwe national monument and its ancient architectural thrills. Never mind the wonders of the mountains and hills of the Eastern Highlands which are said to be beautiful all year round. Black Zimbabweans do not fancy spending a week gazing at the thunderous waters of the falls or the stonework of Great Zimbabwe. No, that is not in their scheme of things.

Zimbabwean men are generally in a state of continuous drunkenness, not drunk with work or other passions, but drunk with real alcohol. A Zimbabwean is either drunk, just about to become drunk or is recovering from drunkenness. Our three states of being, Zimbabwean men, black and white.

Recently two guzzlers epitomised this alcoholic drama by challenging each other to a drinking contest. The scene was a bar in the small southern town of Masvingo. They drank until they collapsed unconscious. They had to be ferried to a hospital where the alcoholic beverages were drained from their veins which contained more alcohol than human blood.

Ask any Zimbabwean about their leisure time and you will get fascinating answers. 'Gazing at the water falling from a cliff is not my idea of enjoying life,' said one business consultant. His company had taken him to Lake Kariba on a leisure boat for three days. There was no shadow of enjoyment on his face when he came back.

In a country whose major housing areas were built mainly for migrant labourers, most Harareans have no other way of 'killing time' except the beerhall, the bar. There is hardly any space in the housing estates or townships for anything creative or relaxing. The houses are crowded like magnified matchboxes dumped without any imagination onto a football pitch. Children have no space even to roll a toy car or run a few paces before they come back with a nose bashed against a wall.

So the man walks away, abandoning the wife and children to their own fate. The ordinary Zimbabwean woman does not have leisure in her agenda of things. If she does, then it is in the hidden agenda rather than the open one. Or if she lives in the city centre, she might eventually ask the maid to take the children into the park on a Sunday afternoon. She might opt for the Hollywood-type soaps abundant in the movie houses of the inner city.

When a Zimbabwean says, 'Let's go for a drink,' he means it. 'Let's have one,' simply means let's start with one each, and continue until we cannot count anymore. Then, the drinking gets rough and the tough get going. In the end, Zimbabweans will always 'have one for the road', but with the many roads of the city 'one for the road' might actually mean a flood.

Zimbabwean weekends, especially month-ends, are days of death. The driver in the other car is likely to be drunk by midday, totally drunk by midnight and hopeless in the early hours of the morning. The pedestrian walking on the pavement or the side of the road is not as sober as he might appear. Go to a Zimbabwean party and see the amount of alcohol assembled in waiting. Then at the end of the party, see the drunken faces, hear the drunken insults and probably witness drunken fights.

'We came out of a war ten years ago, but we still behave so militaristically,' a friend once remarked. We have come out of a war, yes, but the war has not yet come out of us. Maybe it has become a permanent feature of Zimbabweans' cultural existence.

No, this is not to paint Zimbabweans as gun-wielding thugs who drink and drink their feet to liquid before embarking on cowboyish gunfights. No. We consume vast amounts of alcohol and then we dance to our popular music.

Zimbabweans always sing and dance. At the Thomas Mapfumo show the audience is not left out. They sing and dance along with their star who earns himself a new nickname with each album. The all-night *pungwe* (music concert) is a mark of the Zimbabwean entertainment diary every month-end. The dancing and the drinking (not quite reaching that of the gaucho dances of Latin America) swell and the revellers drive home dazed with music, dance and vast amounts of alcohol. After all, Sunday is always there to pick up the bits and pieces. Everything is centered on beer-drinking. After the soccer match, the place to go is the bar. After work, it is the bar. At a party, it is heavy bouts of drinking until people collapse. A party without enough alcohol is a disaster from the outset.

Before even a school is built in any new residential area, the bar is already there, visibly. Schools and clinics might come later. And the names of the beerhalls tell it all — *rambanayi* (go ahead and divorce); *mapitikoti* (place of many petticoats); *manhede* (lying on the back, suggesting the sexual act); *makovhorosi* (booze during lunch break with overall on); *mushayambereko* (one who abandoned child-rearing in pursuit of the joys of alcohol and sex). Beer-drinking and women: the leisure pursuits of Zimbabwean men.

Since independence in 1980 a new leisure invention has arrived. Zimbabweans love their soccer no matter what. But the ageing players, those who played in school long back, are too old or busy for competitive soccer. They now run what are called 'boozers' clubs' whose main mission is to break all the soccer rules. First, there are 30 players instead of the normal 22. And for first aid the injured are treated to mugs of beer. Any player-boozer who feels his throat itching for 'booze' simply walks away to drink in the dust.

If the absence of a library in a community is an indication of illiteracy, then nearly all Zimbabwean communities are illiterate. The word 'library' itself is associated with a school; books are for schoolchildren as they strive to pass their examinations, and if you sit in a bar reading a book, frequenters are not slow to remind you that, 'This is not a schoolroom, it is a bar.'

Charles Mungoshi, my fellow writer, has a reputation for forgetting his books in the bar. But when he goes back the following morning he has always found his books where he has left them. Reading books, for most Zimbabweans, is an activity as solitary as writing them. So they choose to talk.

Ours is a country of married men, not married women. In the bars, only single women appear, to gulp down their share of the drinks, scouting for men. Or the single women, who are 'taken out' by their boyfriends. Married women, no. Bars are rough places where a decent woman should never venture, so the thinking goes. And even during the occasional picnic, or riverside beer-drinking to the accompaniment of music from a small radio, wives are not usually to be found. They do not exist. That is the domain of girlfriends. So the women sit at home knitting, scrubbing the dirty floor, changing nappies and being generally available at home.

Zimbabweans love parties so middle-income mothers have invented their own type of party, the 'kitchen party'. These usually take place on a Saturday afternoon to bid 'farewell to freedom' collectively to a young woman who has braved the storm of marriage. The 'kitchen party' is now on most women's lips, over the phone, in the street. Not the disco.

The disco is also a place for men, and single women who happen either to be in search of a 'catch', as it is called, or have been taken out by their boyfriends. Married women are doomed to stay at home, bored, but resigned to it. 'The man will come back,' the auntie, a traditional adviser, usually consoles the woman. She herself has been through it. She was not divorced because she was able to remain subdued, without protesting.

This type of leisure: 'May it not finish us all until we are, in the name of a bar, *marengenya* (worn out with alcohol)'.

Forsaken by the Gods

If you don't stay bitter
and angry for too long
you might finally salvage
something useful
from the old country.

The Zimbabwean poet Charles Mungoshi wrote these lines many years ago, decrying the plight of the peasant pushed onto poor marginal lands by land-hungry commercial farmers. He was a sprinkle of hope, even in the rubble of death and decay of the marginalised rural lands where rain hardly fell, and if it did the sandy soil refused to yield to human efforts to make it productive.

But today the 'old country' is a symbol of utter death and decay, with carcasses of dead cattle strewn all over the place, and already there are reports of people dying in the grip of the worst drought in Zimbabwe's century-old recorded history.

Nothing 'useful' seems salvageable from this

'old country' in which whispers of death seem the only remnant in that sea of despair.

Back home, my mother feels that, 'There is nothing but death here.' She is in the country, mourning memories by the graves of our ancestors which she cannot desert to come to the city where she could live with her urban children.

But the lure of the city is intense throughout the land as people find some hope in the glitter of the city. This is a hope based on the safety of numbers since it seems there is always something to scrounge in the cities and urban centres.

'Home sweet home?' No, home, as Charles Mungoshi was to write later, is now the

aftermath of an invisible war
a heap of dust and rubble
white immobile heat on the sweltering land.

And the vulture waits for its share of the carrion as the cattle die before the eyes of their hunger-weary owners. Sheep, donkeys — anything that moves faces the grim prospect of slow death by starvation.

It is like in the old folk tales, the stories of massive droughts in the land of the animals, in which the hare and the tortoise devised new survival tricks. This time the tale is not one of fictitious animals but a tale of real human beings, children and mothers, worn out by hunger and thirst, eating anything which is not poison — wild fruit, mountain plants, fruits of the baobab tree ...

In times of crisis, Zimbabweans tend to be superstitious and sceptical about everything. 'This government was not grateful enough to hold thanksgiving rituals, thanking the ancestors for having had a successful liberation war,' says a headman, a traditional leader whose authority has been immensely eroded since independence in 1980. The current leaders instituted new laws which render the traditional leaders powerless, leaving them as mere symbols of power.

As the bulky Vice-President speaks, the countryside smells of death. His own home town, Bulawayo, with nearly one million people, faces the prospect of extinction.

'We are the children of a forsaken god, a god who has also abandoned us,' says a peasant woman visiting the city to beg. She is not quite a beggar like those city beggars sitting on the pavement, singing holy songs to lure coins from passers-by. She is a peasant, haunted by hunger and death, who has had to leave her home and come to the city in search of relatives who can throw a few crumbs her way. The countryside has become unliveable, a desert of death and destruction, this time caused by nature which has harshly decided to punish her own children.

As I talk to the old woman, I see tears welling up in her ageing eyes, her heart heavy as she recalls what might happen to those she left at home. 'My sister is not well and she does not have anything to eat. If nothing happens, she will be dead soon,' the old woman tells me. She is my relative and in me she sees some hope, the thin ray of light which says there must be life in this death.

In the countryside vast tracts of ploughed land lie empty. Nothing ever grows there, not even the hardy traditional crops which give hope to the peasants when the modern crops have let them down.

'You see, these are the lands in which we planted seed,' says a young extension officer pushed out of a job since he has nobody to advise on improved ways of farming. 'Some were lucky to have a few drops of rain, but we were not. If anything germinated, it was soon burnt by the harsh sun,' he explains.

The herd-boys who once sang in the plains, herding cattle, milking the cows and wrestling with the calves, they too have vanished. Instead, there are the scattered white bones of the cattle which die daily. For many years parts of the countryside have been on the verge of a drought with little rain and poor sandy soils from whose heart nothing emerges. Since January 1992 over 4,000 head of cattle have been dying every month in one province alone. Boreholes supplying water to schools have dried up and the headmasters have had no option but to close the schools and send the children home to another drought where they sit and watch their parents rendered powerless.

'The government needs at least 5 million US dollars per month for the drought,' says the Minister of Labour and Social Services. This frightening figure does not include the cost of keeping alive the city of Bulawayo. Zimbabwe's western capital and second largest city is under the shadow of death as its water supplies are only three months from drying up.

Of the country's population of ten million, over 80 per cent depend directly on agriculturally-based industries. By the coming of the rains in November a large number of workers will have lost their means of earning a decent livelihood. And if it fails to rain again, many more human deaths will intensify the pain on the many faces of peasants and workers across the nation.

'It cannot rain properly anymore.' I remember my mother's words as we talked about the drought and its victims. 'We have done many things to defile the land. People have cut trees which our ancestors forbade us to cut, they have left the carcasses of crocodiles and hippos in the open,' she once told me. Yes, she might not quite know how to preserve the vegetation in the way of learned scholars and academics but she bemoans the human insensitivity to the balance of life which has now been turned into the imbalance of death.

'Power Blackout Looms over Zimbabwe' screams a newspaper headline. It is the story, not fictitious, of how a whole country might find itself without electricity as the water levels of Lake Kariba continue to dwindle. Zimbabwe generates its power from the hydroelectric station on that vast lake, but the lake faces one of its leanest years ever, with the water levels expected to drop lower than the power-generating turbines on the dam wall.

Meanwhile, horrific scenes of the drought continue to invade our television screens as ministers address rallies before giving food hand-outs to the desolate-looking peasants. New crimes of theft of maize meal come alive as young men and women confront the possibility of death by starvation. In the city too the thieves are more daring, robbing banks at gun-point, one of the last desperate deeds of a country facing unemployment and a visible natural disaster.

As I yearn for the seasonal cry of the cicada just before the rains in November, the mournful city tells me of many deaths of peasants in the countryside. When the raindrops come, there will be many funerals to tell how the drought made life so cheap. As cheap as the air we all breathe.

Zimbabwe:
'If You Don't Stay Bitter
Too Long'

'Don't Kill Our Farms' reads a sticker on a farmer's car, a voice of protest at the manner in which the government has been controlling prices of farm produce for the past twelve years. The pressure is now on the government to desist from any further control. And nature too has highlighted the drama in this land of maize fields and hills endowed with a large variety of minerals.

Since independence in 1980 Zimbabwe has upheld a record as one of the few African countries to feed itself entirely, prompting Zimbabweans to refer proudly to their country as 'The Grain Basket of Southern Africa'.

But 1992 destroyed that myth, with nature taking its toll as the rains refused to fall, leaving bare fields and broken hearts throughout the country.

Today, after the usual ferocious thunder and lightning, Zimbabwe — 'The House of Stone' — is once again bright. 1993 arrived with leafy hills and heavily clouded skies. Now the birds can sing and the crickets chirp all night. The fields are lush green, delivering hope to the farmers who spent 1992 in gloom and despair. This lush green belies the experiences lying not so deep in the memory of the nation. Only six months ago one could have easily mistaken the whole country for a desert. Then the birds were quiet, the crickets were dead and the bare rocky hills dominated the misery of the drought-stricken countryside as they imposed their will on the eyes of the nation, defying the memory of the plentiful harvests of the past decade.

'You see, our crops are finished, our cattle dead and our children are already fainting in class every day,' said an old peasant farmer to me as we walked across his bare fields. That was early in 1992 at the height of what should have been the rainy season. The rains had not fallen and the faces of the peasants and commercial farmers looked worn out with anxiety. The old man would talk about praying for the rain, echoing the national religious leaders who had swarmed into churches in order to plead with the gods, all in vain.

Much as 1992 was 'annus horribilis' for the Queen of England, it was the year of the dust bowl for Zimbabwe, a year in which Southern Africa's grain basket became, as Charles Mungoshi had predicted, 'a heap of dust and rubble'.

Nearly one million head of cattle perished during

the 1991-92 rainless season. It was as if Charles Mungoshi's words, 'The sharp-nosed vulture already smells of carrion,' had prophesied this tragic dust bowl long before it touched our landscape.

Indeed there was 'carrion' as the cattle, the usually resilient goats, sheep, donkeys and wild animals died, leaving skeletons strewn across the plains and the hillsides. The cow that went to the nearby dry river to sip at the dry mud collapsed and died. The ox too, the strong one, slept under the shade of a tree while the harsh sun drained it of all energy until it could not rise.

Besides loss of draught power, Zimbabwe was, for the first time, unable to meet its export quota of 9,100 tonnes of beef a year to the European Community. Thus the national revenue shrank, forcing the Cold Storage Commission to close several of its abattoirs.

'It will take us another four years to rebuild the national herd,' says National Farmers Union President, Gary Magadzire. Experts think the farmers will need over 200 million Zimbabwean dollars to undertake the revival of the national herd to its pre-drought levels of two million head of cattle. Couple that with the stiff European Community veterinary requirements and the fear is that Europe might begin looking elsewhere in order to meet the Zimbabwean beef quota.

Crops wilted too as the weary eyes of peasants looked on, all under the bleaching sun, turning everything into Charles Mungoshi's 'white immobile heat on the sweltering land'. Production of maize, the staple food of the country, dropped from an annual two million tonnes to a mere 50,000 tonnes in the 1991-92 season. They had to import grain from the European Community and the Americas at prices much higher than local yields had given to the farmers. Charles Mungoshi wrote many years ago about bitterness and the sour taste of the harsh life of the Zimbabwean countryside. He was writing about the dead countryside, a place where death abounded. In such a 'home' hope is difficult to sustain.

For Zimbabwe, 1992 was the year of 'dust' and 'rubble' as the countryside bled. Everything bled. The trees as they died, the cattle, the starving people as they waited for sprinkles of drought relief food from seemingly never-arriving government trucks. And when the lorries arrived, there would be announcements of new cuts in the amount of maize meal, invoking the anger of the peasants and small-scale farmers. The usually docile peasants are reported to have assaulted, sometimes fatally, the government officials who distributed food.

Over a million tonnes of grain were imported as the citizens began to ask question: how did we come to this? Allegations of bad advice from World Bank officials surface. It was too expensive for Zimbabwe to store large amounts of grain, they said, so the grain was sold to Zambia to curtail the political reper-cussions of maize-meal shortage during Kaunda's last days in power. Friends must come to each other's rescue. Then there was a revision of memory, farmers remembering those years of 'bumper harvests' when

Nove Muchachi, the then Deputy Minister of Agriculture, chided farmers for growing too much maize. His advice was for farmers to opt for cotton, soya beans, flowers, sunflowers, tobacco and non-consumable crops which would earn Zimbabwe the fetishistically worshipped hard currency.

Faced with the low prices of maize, the farmers, especially white commercial farmers, shifted to horticulture and game ranching.

In 1992 Zimbabwean farmers exported 200 million Zimbabwean dollars' worth of flowers to the European Community, especially to The Netherlands, a rise from the previous year. The horticultural industry was not affected by the drought and the 1993 season is likely to yield even higher figures.

Game ranching has caught the farmers' imagination, with almost every commercial farmer putting aside a portion of his farm for wild animals, and ostrich has recently become a delicacy in Zimbabwean hotels.

'At least fifteen international buyers from Europe have shown interest in Zimbabwe ostrich meat,' says a marketing manager of Copro, a company in charge of the marketing drive for ostrich meat, skins, feathers and eggs.

Tobacco also enjoyed a glorious year as the farmers, mainly those in the commercial sector, continue to report higher yields. In 1992 tobacco farmers exported one billion dollars' worth of the crop. Tobacco is not affected by the drought since it flourishes in low rainfall areas and on sandy soils.

Alongside other factors, this shift to cash crops

contributed to the 'dust bowl' I mentioned earlier.

Zimbabwe normally exports cotton to the European Community. But the 1991-92 season saw a drastic drop in cotton yields. Both pests and the drought reduced the cotton yield from 180,000 tonnes in 1990-91 to a mere 50,000 during the 1991-92 season. Already there is fear that the clothing industry is close to collapse. Workers in the industry have been retrenched as the clothing manufacturers fight to survive.

1993 is different, however. The green fields and valleys leave a smell of hope in the air. Talk of a 'bumper harvest' is rife in the mouths of agricultural economists. But we will need another two or three years of good rains to recover, they caution.

Finance Minister Bernard Chizero has finally bowed to a heavy World Bank-IMF programme to restructure the economy. That means drastic devaluation of the local currency under pressure from the donor community which had always argued that the Zimbabwean currency was overvalued. In 1990 one US dollar was equivalent to about 3.5 Zimbabwean dollars. By March 1993 one US dollar was equivalent to nearly seven Zimbabwean dollars. Faced with that burden on the national currency, inflation continues to rise, coupled with high unemployment as more and more people lose their jobs due to the closure of factories and non-competitive industries.

Zimbabwe is one large farmland inhabited by nearly eleven million people earning their livelihood from the soil in one way or the other. Any serious drought like the recent one kills everything, even hope.

Prospects for trade are bright only in the crops and commodities which are not consumable. That is the danger of a cash economy in an agricultural country, a country where anyone who is not able to feed himself from his own piece of land is derided and mocked.

Unfortunately a Third World country like Zimbabwe is up against the wall of world trade. Prices of commodities are determined by the buyers rather than the sellers. They call it an open market economy whose effects have meant the total destruction of the economically weak by the strong.

Flowers will continue to be flown to Europe. And tobacco too, the cancer-causing smoke. But people do not eat flowers and tobacco. None the less, they are the nation's hard-cash earners, hence the shift to those crops and neglect of food crops.

The politics of food and the worship of the fetish of 'hard currency' still linger in the mind. I cannot but hear the words of the Algerian lawyer Mohammed Redjanui as he described the deterioration of terms of trade as 'the new forms of slavery of modern times'.

Willy Brandt, the former West German Chancellor, observed the need for profound changes in international economics, for new insights into the justice of word trade so that the Third World will not continue to be the supplier of cheap raw materials and the recipient of highly priced manufactured products from the developed world.

'The primary objective of development is to lead to self-fulfilment and creative partnership in the use of a nation's productive forces and its full human potential,' remarked Brandt. He was appealing for a different type of trade between countries, the type of trade which accepts the cultural worth of the other and so gives dignity to all participants.

All is not lost, though droughts come and go, natural and human disasters impinge on the visions of the South with every setting sun. Developing countries continue to prevail on us to change our economies to suit their needs, and wars too continue to be fed from the steady supply of highly sophisticated weapons and war technology from the North.

But all is not lost. The only weapon which abounds in countries of the South is hope as the sound of grazing cattle reminds us that life is in the 'newly turned soil' where the seeds of hope also germinate.

Once Upon a Democracy - Zimbabwe

Once upon a time, a chief sat at court with his advisors and any member of the chieftaincy who chose to attend. Arguments and issues were tossed in all directions across the floor. Everyone saluted the chief before reprimanding or praising him. Court poets recited the successes and failures of the chief's regime. Meanwhile the chief listened, inwardly moved for fear he might restrict the participation of the people. A statement was inevitable as the debates became more heated than ever before. No solution was in sight.

Then a stranger with a load on his head and his feet itching for their tiring, far-away destination appeared on the horizon. 'Call that man,' the chief's advisor told a young man. The stranger was summoned to the court where he sat and saluted the court and the elders. Immediately, the advisor briefed him without bias on the nature of the issues under discussion.

'As a passer-by, what do you think?' Whereupon the man humbly gave his considered views. All sides to the debate listened in disbelief, stunned but convinced by the stranger's new perceptions of the issue at hand. The day was done. Discussion ended in consensus and a pinch of objectivity.

That was centuries ago when village life meant that everyone knew almost everyone else. This is 1994 and Zimbabwe is no longer a chieftaincy where anyone could walk into the seat of power to listen and to be heard. Zimbabwe is a modern state. Colonialism destroyed most of the traditional institutions that would have been a basis for a new modern democracy. In their place colonialism put a harsh police machinery, repressive laws to maintain 'order' by force and restrictive media laws of defamation which make journalists wield the pen in fear.

In Zimbabwe the elected President is viewed as the fountain of national wisdom, the national identity. His goal is to 'develop' all as they 'rally' behind him and his team of appointed ministers.

So far, nearly the entire team of ministers has remained in office for the past fourteen turbulent years. One wonders whether or not there is a system for the democratic evaluation of their performance.

The voices of the powerful are largely heard through government-controlled newspapers, state-owned radio (with four channels) and a semi-government-owned news agency. It is not easy for other news agencies to sell their news to newspapers and magazines in Zimbabwe.

There is a Ministry of Information whose task is to control and regulate the flow of information to the public. Information 'controls' minds of the citizenry in any country. In the end the dominant point of view becomes that of the government, whose view must prevail even if it might be false or warped. Control of hearts and minds. The people must not be confused by 'disgruntled elements', the government seems to say. Those elements threaten national unity and development. So only recently there was a political stir when two senior Ndebele politicians in the ruling party claimed government institutions practised 'tribalism'.

The broadcasting station, major newspapers and the only news agency are government-controlled. There is hardly a day when the President is not headline news of one sort or another. Government ministers and powerful people's speeches are the news, not the events which prompted those speeches. At the same time, the people are censored by illiteracy, hence the abuse of the mysterious radio voice to indoctrinate them into a state of passivity.

As a result journalism has become the art of summarising ministerial speeches. Debate and critical analysis died years back. In the 1980s this style of journalism was called 'development journalism' which was to compete with 'sensational journalism' of the West. Later, when the phrase got stale, it surfaced as 'constructive criticism' when prescribed by those same powerful figures. In both eras, the press continued to be diluted and many critical journalists left to become public relations officers for multinationals and parastate organisations.

The few non-government newspapers and magazines cry under the weight of one burden or another. Advertising space dwindles as private concerns fear to be associated with the wrong side of the economy. The government's bureaucracy makes it impossible for 'independent' journalists to obtain information on the day-to-day goings on in government. In such circumstances accountability fades away and public officials go about their daily work knowing only too well that no one is watching them critically.

During the vicious years of apartheid in South Africa the voices of the independent press reminded the world that ugliness was being institutionalised in that country. Media revelations of the excesses of apartheid shook the world's consciences into action. The press refused to be gagged, even by apartheid's harsh media laws. Come majority rule and the South African press might fall into the temptation of not daring to criticise the same people who symbolised their ideals during the years of repression. 'We might be blamed for not supporting national unity and development,' they might say as a lame excuse for not obeying their consciences.

Today, the Zimbabwean press lacks vigour and vision. Major media channels concern themselves with full coverage of President Robert Mugabe's 'successful' tours overseas, but the people have instituted a new medium: rumour and gossip. President Mugabe himself publicly admitted that Harare was the capital of rumours. The rumour press operates from public drinking places, private clubs, the streets, private gatherings like parties and meetings.

Whenever scandals surface, few in the government-controlled media dare to investigate them, and if they do, they do so at their peril. The late Willie Musaruwa, one of Zimbabwe's best journalists, detained for eleven years by the Smith government, was summarily dismissed from his position as editor of the *Sunday Mail* in 1985 for publishing a story the government did not like. So journalists who write in fear of their masters indulge in the final act of censorship – self-censorship. Donor agencies and governments feature daily on television and in the newspapers, pouring their begged-for money into our national coffers. Thus we become a nation of beggars whose hands are fully stretched to receive every cent from the wealthy nations of the North. No word about our national identities, our aspirations and perceptions, nothing. In the Zimbabwean media, our faces are blurred. We are mere masks performing in a farce from whose authorship we have been removed.

Praise singers, flatterers and sycophants have a field day. The right of access to information, the right of every citizen to participate in national debates, is relegated to the dustbin.

Ask any leader of the so-called 'opposition parties' what their experience is in trying to get a simple permit to hold a political meeting. I call ours a 'masked democracy', something which gives the stranger only a resemblance, which is not the real thing. Democracy does not mean fourteen or twenty registered political parties. It means participation at the lowest and weakest level of society.

Only informed citizens make effective democrats. Democracy is basically the right of the citizen to be right and to be wrong. It is based on the right to choose even if a citizen makes wrong choices. The right to choose entails a continual search for alternatives. The consensus of the old village is no longer enough. In its place should be the accommodation of differences and different approaches to life and death.

In Zimbabwe, deprivation of the right to choose is called 'guided democracy', a notion which assumes that the truth is found at the centre of power. As far as I can see, the truth is indeed found in the individual voice, the faintest voice in the land, the voice of a dispossessed citizen who invents new language to describe his or her new damned conditions. Thus democracy ceases to be just a five-yearly vote-casting farce without anything in between. Democracy becomes continual dialogue in which all the layers of society, individuals and communities, stand up for their rights and are listened to. Democracy can never thrive in a political monologue in which the leaders, like rain gods, pour messages on the heads of disempowered individuals and communities.

At the centre of this multi-faceted dialogue is the right to be informed and the right to inform without undue interference from the powerful.

Epilogue:
As I Wrote About My Country

The land of one's birth is always non-existent, in the heart and the blood, being ignored. For many weeks now I have had a dialogue with my own land in a newspaper column published in a far-away country, sharing my breath, the pulse of my heart, with so many readers whom I would never meet. It was such a joy to meet without meeting, to meet on the black dots and white spaces of a newspaper. Such is that sad joy which sometimes makes one want to shed joyful tears. Sweet sadness.

Sweet sadness. I saw the tears on the faces of the village women out there among the hills and valleys where I was born. My mother, too, is among them, crying and laughing with them. And here I was, writing about the village women left alone by men who escaped to the city to live in the anticipated joy of searching for themselves as they stared at the glitter of the city lights which only gave them a gleam of hope but not employment. Families torn apart by the new migration, the lure of what my fellow poet Musa Zimunya has called 'country dawns and city lights'.

What makes for a national identity, a national personality, or a national psyche, I do not know, but I have, in the experience of writing these essays, heard the sounds of the birds, the animals, the happy and sad children, the elders singing their way home or the dead recalled by the living. I have seen the Zimbabwean personality in the flooded river, in the hills, in the boulders which balance on other boulders, in the city lights which glitter with a mixture of hope and despair, in the thunder and bang of car accidents on the highways of my country.

I heard the personality of the land in the songs of the musicians, in the songs of the little cicadas which sing their way to death, to life. It is only when I wrote about these events and these features of our lives that I realised they are also part of a bigger personality, a bigger dance in which we are mere ants with small voices that come together to form this other bigger dance whose end or beginning no one knows.

Don't we all write or talk in order to search for ourselves, to locate ourselves in time and space? The essays were part of that process too, for me, for readers and even for those who did not read them.

'We are chroniclers of our time,' says a voice in me. But another voice answers me, 'Time is also our chronicler.' Time and I have this implicit agreement that we will respect each other's laws. The laws of life and death blended, fused together.

And I have respected that agreement in poetry, in novels, in essays, in newspaper articles. I hope time will say to me, thank you for reporting me aright, in the words of a doubt-torn Prince Hamlet. And time and I will shake hands, time as history, me embracing the earth in that final departure, death.

As I wrote these essays, I woke up to many things, to my life. I began to think more about the contrasts, the similarities of the face of this land, these cities which are like little monsters borrowed from another century, implanted here without recognising the land, the hills and rivers where they have been planted. The houses, those skyscrapers, those gaping roads, they are sometimes sore on the eye, sometimes a healthy escape from the vagaries of the environment out there in the countryside where the women go for miles to fetch a drop of water for the crying children while the vulture waits without despair for its share of the flesh of the land.

In other words, the essays gave me a time for a further dialogue with myself. As a writer, sometimes there is a temptation to engage in dialogue with the characters I create. That is at the expense of dialogue with myself. For, as I wrote, I began to ask many questions, old questions about the contradictions, the pangs, the pains which we have, as a nation, as a city, as communities, the pain endured as we carve our psychological and emotional landscape.

I have been learning to read more and more the words written on our emotional map, the mind we created from the experience of many years of war. The essays were at the centre, refreshing my mind, drawing my vision from the distant to the nearby, the immediate which I found has more to teach us than the grand visions created by multitudes of social philosophies of life that burden our clarity without us knowing it.

Were I a good church-goer, I would change some of the holy son's words in that old prayer to 'Our Father who art in heaven, sharpen our social perceptions.' For, when we drag our feet, busy with the big and small issues of our daily lives, we become mere shadows of what we could be. We blunt our social perceptions, forgetting the face of the earth, the dust which blows into our eyes, the flies which cause us disease, the tiny loads which create our heavy burdens. Our social perceptions die and we follow the tedium of life, being dragged along, dying, breathing our way to our graves. What more does one need except a chance to sniff around, living, dying, but with a smile on one's face? The years of solitude have to be fought with all the imaginative ammunition I can muster. To write is to fight.

Yes, experience, we always look for experience, the flowers of life. They might be red or white, rich flavours or bad ones, those that irritate us out of our life. But they are experience all the same. So, now I can hear the sirens of power, I can remember the paraphernalia of power, I can see the land and the city staring at each other in futile argument. I can see them because I have been writing about them for all these years, I have spoken to them in the language they gave me for these essays. Dream and experience, life.

As for the reader, I hope my words celebrated our encounter as we invaded each other's minds, not with spears and guns but with words. To read is to argue, to brew the vital liquor of life so that writers can be jerked out of the many blurred visions which they take for granted.

GIFTS
Nuruddin Farah

'One of the finest contemporary African novelists'
SALMAN RUSHDIE

'Every gift has a personality — that of its giver,' writes Nuruddin Farah. Indeed, the exchange of presents, whether longed-for or unexpected, wanted or unwanted, lies at the heart of human affairs, and both giver and receiver are changed by the gift relationship.

In this beguiling tale of a Somali family and a growing love affair, Nuruddin Farah explores not only the way presents bind relatives and friends together but also how 'gifts' from the industrialised to the 'Third World' create similar ties — and debts. Engaging, humorous and enigmatic, Nuruddin Farah goes to the very heart of one of the most vexed questions of our time.

'Nuruddin Farah is one of the real interpreters of experience on our troubled continent. His insight goes deep, beyond events, into the sorrows and joys, the frustrations and achievements of our lives. His prose finds the poetry that is there.'
NADINE GORDIMER

Nuruddin Farah, who was born in Baidoa, Somalia, in 1945, is one of Africa's most acclaimed writers. His novels include *Maps*, *Sardines* and *Sweet and Sour Milk*, which won the 1980 English Speaking Union Literary Award; the recipient of a number of international prizes, his work has been translated into more than a dozen languages.